11 11

THE
AWAKENING
CODE

CHRISTINE NIETO

ISBN: 978-1-968970-71-0 Paperback
ISBN: 978-1-968970-72-7 Ebook

Rev. date: 09/17/2025

CONTENTS

SECOND EDITION SHAMBHALA AND WAR PIGS

How does your light shine?

The cover shows 2 pathways created in the center by each 11. One pathway driven by the emotion of love and one pathway driven by fear. The road to Shambhala was written by Daniel Moore and released in1973 by three dog night and B.W. Stevenson. The song's lyrics say "How does your light shine in the halls of Shambhala." Shambhala is a spiritual kingdom characterized by love, peace and happiness, a utopian society driven by love. War Pigs is depicted as the pathway driven by fear. A dystopian society resulting from the evils of war. It was released in 1970 by Black Sabbath. The years they were released and the words are typical of the sentiments expressed in many songs written by many young artists during the 60's and early 70's. Many of these artists could be referred to as hippies.

Hippies are rarely if ever recognized for the level of consciousness and spirituality they demonstrated by the songs that were released in response to the Viet Nam war the draft and the status quo in general. In fact hippies are often referred to as dirty sex crazed druggies. For many years that generalization overshadowed the true nature of the counterculture movement. Refer Madness, a movie that came out in the 1930's was responsible for perpetuating the lies that depicted marijuana use as a dangerous gateway drug that led to murder, suicide, hallucinations and a decent into madness. It was a propaganda film revolving around the events that occurred after high school students were lured into smoking marijuana.

I intend to demonstrate that for the most part the hippies were on a spiritual path. The fact that there were over a half a million people at Woodstock smoking pot with not one incidence of violence is testimony to the fact that smoking the peace pipe does not lead to violence or madness. It seems that the powers that be will go to great lengths to undermine the use of any mind altering plants. Plants that grow naturally and were put here by intelligent design. Many of which can be instrumental in achieving enlightenment and for mental health issues as well.

In the case of Timothy Leary, he was a psychologist, who lectured regularly at Harvard. He was a genius and philosopher. He was a brave soul who offered a way into the future. He is truly a historical figure who was brave enough to promote the use of LSD in the 60's. He coined the phrase turn on tune in and drop out. He endorsed the use of psychedelic drugs for use in mental health issues. He wanted the whole world to turn on to acid or LSD. He believed that the ecstasy of LSD under supervision of a guide, could be beneficial to the user. After being called the most dangerous man alive, by President Nixon and run out of the country, it turns out he was right. These psychedelic plants like psilocybin (magic mushrooms) are now being used to treat PTSD as well as other mental ailments. I found out that the reason cows are sacred to many people in India, it is because the mushrooms grow under their poop, and are responsible for facilitating enlightenment.

It is well known that the government (CIA) were doing experiments with LSD (acid) as a truth serum. These experiments were referred to as MKUltra. The government realized that the acid trip was capable of causing healing and perhaps on a global level if world leaders and others were to make use of it. The powers that be weren't having none of it. They would not endorse anything that might bring about a more peaceful human being and ultimately a more peaceful world.

Timothy Leary ended up being caught with two marijuana roaches in his car and sentenced to 30 years in prison. Within the confines of jail he continued to write books. The powers that be made an example out of him. President Nixon turned a brilliant philosopher and psychologist, a way shower for peace in to the most dangerous man alive.

The novel entitled Mary's Mosaic, by Peter Janney, demonstrates another successful attempt to end any notions of a peaceful world. Apparently President Kennedy had found a soul mate in one of his affairs. He had fallen in love with a socialite who had spent time with Timothy Leary and had made use of LSD. It is said that she turned President Kennedy on to marijuana and possibly LSD. They had a vision for world peace. They were both murdered.

It seems the powers that be will go to great lengths to keep us in fear and to suppress any influential people that would endorse a more peaceful approach to world affairs. From day one we are taught to fear. For example think of how babies were greeted upon being born. A slap on the bottom. I'm not sure if that practice is still used, however the practice of cutting a boy baby's penis as in circumcision, is a common practice, at least here in the United States. I think the practice is totally unnatural and cruel. It is as if the medical field does not believe in intelligent design. We go along with this torture like sheeple.

Ever since I can remember there has been something to fear. In grade school we had drills that had us under our desks in case of nuclear war. Many people are in fear on a daily basis. The fear of survival is ever present. Can I pay the rent, feed my family? These are common fears that linger in the psyche of millions of people. It doesn't have to be that way. We can "shoe the children with no shoes on their feet." We can "house the people living in the street." There is a solution. Those words from another song from the early 70's. Stevie Miller and his band knew that we can solve these problems with love.

It is plain to see that this nation is not providing an atmosphere whereby the population is thriving. We live in a society that does not provide an environment that fosters self-actualization. This is true for most of the world. I intend to give evidence to the idea that the powers that be want a dysfunctional chaotic world filled with war and suffering. The war pigs have been influencing mankind forever. Like the song says, "Evil minds that plot destruction, Sorcerer of deaths destruction." Black Sabbath nailed it with that song.

War, what is it good for absolutely nothing. Edwin Starr nailed it with that song. War is not good for humans but there is a group of beings that run the world, and war is good for them. This group of beings are not fully Human. There evil deeds have been going on for centuries. Ancient aliens have been influencing our planet for centuries. These evil beings live off of our negative energy. They are responsible for introducing money religion and technology to our planet. The love of money is the root of all evil. They are in fact the money lovers. They could throw billions in the toilet and never miss it. It is not the acquisition of money that turns them on, but rather the withholding from us that makes their boat float. That is because they thrive on negative energy. Humans thrive and blossom on the energy of love, but it's quite the opposite for these beings. These beings thrive off of the negative energy that is created with war and the struggle that most people endure to survive. Einstein said that everything is energy and that is all there is energy.

We were never meant to worry the way that people do. When I think of all the worries people seem to find and how they're in a hurry to complicate their minds by chasing after money and things that can't come true. The grass roots sang that song and they were right. This isn't the way to live. This is not the way things should be.

It is easy to draw parallels between Native American tribes and the hippies. Native Americans were known to smoke the peace pipe and so were the hippies. The powers that be were well aware of the side effects of marijuana and other hallucinogenic plants on a person's psychic. It is hard to get your war on if people are feeling peaceful. Peyote and psilocybin (magic mushrooms) are known to be mind-expanding especially when done in a spiritual manner. Not as a party drug. Intention is everything. Psilocybin (magic mushrooms), are now being used to treat PTSD, alcoholism, and other mental issues. These substances are known to promote enlightenment. They are known to help to open the third eye, (pineal gland). I read that that is why cows are sacred in parts of India because the magic mushrooms grow under the cows' poop. I found it interesting that the jewel in the center of the forehead is symbolic of the third eye being opened, thus enlightenment.

The Natives were led by their spiritual leaders who were known to use peyote. Of course the powers that be are going to be threatened by mind expanding drugs that show the way to loving one another and the earth. They can't bring on the war machine if psychedelic drugs that promote peace are legal and not stigmatized by lies such as those told in refer madness. The Native Americans had to be portrayed as savages, that had to be conquered. They referred to it as Manifest Destiny. The ideology that god had given Americans the land all the way to the Pacific Ocean and that it was their right and duty to settle in it. So it was the introduction of the root of all evil (money). It now takes precedence over Mother Earth. Native Americans had their healers that used herbs and other natural remedies. Big Pharma wouldn't have a chance if we all depended on natural healers. There are numerous medicinal uses for marijuana that have been suppressed, by the powers that be.

I am reminded of the song Cherokee Nation by Paul Revere and the Raiders, 1971. They took the whole Cherokee Nation put us on this reservation. Took away our way of life, tomahawk and the bow and knife. Took away our native tongue taught their English to our young. And the beads we made by hand are now days made in Japan. But maybe someday when they learn the Cherokee nation will return.

Hippies and Native Americans had similar beliefs in that Mother Earth was sacred. Now the earth the air the water and the food have all been compromised for the root of all evil. Natives did not have money so they never fought a war for some deep dark political objective. We were warned about the danger of the military industrial complex by President Eisenhower.

It seemed that a vortex opened up and poured out universal wisdom into the consciousness of so many young artists that lived in and around Laurel Canyon in the 60' and 70's. So many songs and bands came out of that canyon. Those young artists did psychedelic drugs together, wrote songs together, they opened up their 3rd eye, they wrote mildly political songs underscored by love. In short they opened their minds and looked to their souls. Those words come from the song Crystal Blue Persuasion, by Tommy James and the Shondells. Bands like The Eagles, Crosby Stills Nash and Young, Mamas and the Papas, artists like Joni Mitchell, Jim Morrison, Frank Zappa, Jackson Brown Linda Ronstadt, and many others made music there on that canyon. We need a new age revival for our survival. And, maybe the Cherokee Nation will return.

ABOUT THE BOOK

Christine will explain how she began to search for answers to an ongoing series of mysterious co-incidences that began after the death of her son, who died on 11 11. It was after her son's death that she began to notice seeing 11 11 every time she looked at the clock, or anything that involved numbers. She along with other close members of her family began to be experiencers of the phenomena as well. She then learned that many people are part of this experience. The 11 11 phenomena is also referred to as the Awakening Code. The best way to describe the phenomena is that people begin noticing 11 11 everywhere. 11 or 111 are also part of the puzzle as many people see all three combinations.

The author will explain that there is symbolic meaning regarding the 11 11 phenomena within one of the Mayan temples, called the Temple of the Descending God.

In the book the author shares what she believes are clues given to her, as well as a particular mathematical clue given to everyone. The author points out the relevance of Einstein's quote "the language god wrote the universe in was math." She applies this theory to the mathematical clue that has been given to everyone, in an effort to wake them up. The author reminds us that music is based on mathematical scales, and it is also the universal language. The author includes some mysterious looking photos from the Denver International Airport in the book, that provide evidence of both the problem as well as the solution for world peace today.

She points out that Nikola Tesla said that "we are to the universe as the wave is to the ocean." Part of the whole. The author will explain that we are all part of the universal mind or the universal consciousness.

The author will share with the reader how the ending of the Mayan Calendar marked the end of one age, and the beginning of the Age of Aquarius. She reminds the reader of the song made popular in the 1960s entitled "Aquarius/ Let the Sunshine In". She hopes to push mankind forward into working together as one to bring about harmony and understanding sympathy and trust abounding as the song suggests.

She points to the fact that Einstein and Ghandi both said if 2% of the population meditated on peace at the same time, we would change our reality.

She goes on to explain that the hippies don't get enough credit for the spiritual element to being a hippy. The author believes that many of the songs of the 60's and 70's demonstrated that aspect of that generation. She goes on to say that hippies were instrumental in ending the draft and ultimately the Viet Nam war.

She will explain why she believes in alien lifeforms and why we can't for the most part see them. She will explain why she believes we have been genetically altered to be disconnected with the idea that we are all part of the universal consciousness and the idea that we are all one. The author will explain how it is possible that we have been genetically programmed to receive only a small amount of information that is available through years of programming and manipulation by the powers that be. She points out how various clues at the DIA point towards the idea of secret societies and their alien connection and the sinister agenda that has been a strong influence in our current collective experience on this planet, as well as the past. She hopes to awaken the reader to the idea that we are far more powerful than we have been led to believe. The author hopes to influence the open-minded person to connect the dots as she has and come to the conclusion that we are not alone.

FOREWORD

My love for truth outweighs my fear of offending you

My intention for writing the book is to explain the Awakening Code. In an effort to do this I have to explain what it is to wake up. Waking up involves the idea that we have been living in a matrix. We must realize that our reality has been manipulated by evil forces. For centuries the human race has been manipulated by evil beings and has been controlled by sinister beings that live off of the negative energy created by our struggle to exist in this chaotic world. For this group of controllers, it's not the acquisition of wealth that feeds their hunger, it is the negative energy that is created by our struggle to exist. Einstein said, "Everything is energy and that's all there is." Our current system does not provide the environment for self-actualization. I would not describe our economic system as a thriving one. I say this because of the ongoing wars, homelessness, starvation and degradation of the planet. Of course, some people are privileged. And unfortunately, privilege is when you think something is not a problem because it's not a problem for you personally. I would like to remind people that Nikola Tesla said, "We are to the universe as a wave is to the ocean." A part of the whole. We are all connected.

It seems that no matter who is running the country, nothing ever gets better. Left wing, right wing–same bird.. We must wake up and realize that our perceptions have been hijacked by the powers that be. By this I mean they have used **fear** as a tool to manipulate us and keep our collective vibrational frequencies on a low level. Like the song "Waiting for the World to Change" says, "When they own the information, they can bend it all they want." I will explain why we can no longer wait for the world to change. We are in the Age of Aquarius and a time of synchronicities. A spiritual awakening is occurring in human culture and is marked by co-incidences. I first learned of this awakening when I read the Celestine Prophesies. It was not until the death of my son on 11 11 that I began to experience co-incidences that the book refers to in the first insight.

Another tool that has been used to manipulate us is **religion.** Religion demands that we have faith that there is a god outside of us that we must pray to and ask him to fix things for us. People have been praying for centuries and it hasn't happened yet. A thousand years later and the suffering and wars continue. Often times in in the name of god wars happen. As well as other atrocities. I have offended many people when I point out that there is no god outside of ourselves. Logic and reason would support my statement. Faith in a god outside of ourselves defies logic, and reason. In this book I will introduce proof through ontological mathematics that god exists within all of us and that we are all a fractural part of the light but we all come from the same beam. The sun. I will introduce proof that god is the light, the sun and we are all part of it. Carl Sagan said, "we are all made of star stuff." Carl Sagan also said, "God for you is where you sweep away all the mysteries of the world, all the challenges to our intelligence. You simply turn your mind off and say God did it." I am reminded of the Woodstock song by Crosby Stills Nash and Young. These particular lyrics ring a bell with me, just as so many other songs of the counter culture. I am referring to these lyrics. We are stardust we are golden, we are million-year-old carbon and we've got to get ourselves back to the garden.

Religion involves the idea that an invisible supreme being created us and is overseeing the entire world and Jesus will return someday and thus the rapture. The truth is that the only way things will change is when enough of us wake up and get off of our knees and take our power back. It is up to us to change the way things are. The Christ consciousness must be awakened in enough of us to create a critical mass. That number is needed to ascend on a collective level. In order for us to manifest on this dimension, there has to be both positive and negative energies for us to manifest. A duality, yin and yang. We as humans are the ground for positive and negative energy, that's how we manifest. The idea is for us to collectively raise our vibrations so that we may ascend to another dimension where we can all live in a more peaceful world much like a paradise. The temple of god dwells within all of us and we can do this.

I would like to point out that Meditation is a tool that can be useful in uncovering the third eye. Meditation is the act of going within to that point of consciousness where god individualizes in each of us.

So, for us, we have to have enough good, good, good vibrations on a collective level to ascend to a place where love will steer the stars so to speak. Like the words to the song Aquarius says. Quantum physics points out that our thoughts create our reality and our collective thoughts create our collective reality. Much like a grand thought. Thoughts are vibrational waves. Nikola Tesla said that if you want to understand the universe, think energy, vibration and frequency. We must raise our vibrations on a collective level.

The question is how do we raise our vibrations on a collective level? We must all face our shadow selves. In other words, we must raise our own vibrations by cleaning up our thought forms, since thoughts create our reality. There is a popular new age motto, that dates back to Plato, and the Emerald Tablets. The motto that I am referring to is "what is above so below."

Another way to put it is, "We are a microcosm of the macrocosm." Based on that idea we have to face the negative aspect of ourselves before we can change the world. We have to change our thought patterns and thus our behaviors before we can change the world. Since our thoughts create our reality, we must change the way we think. Moreover, we must forgive ourselves for our transgressions. We must change ourselves, before we can change the world.

At this particular time each and every one of us is going through the dark night of the soul. If we are not, then we should make a conscious effort to change the way we think, in an effort to heal the world. We must face the fact that we have all been toxic in our various relationships and encounters. The point is recognizing it and raising those the vibrations of our thoughts and behaviors and forgive yourself and forgive those who trespass against us. Forgiveness is Divine. Remember that we are designed yin and yang. If we don't practice forgiveness it creates a clog in the artery of Divine energy. Not only have we have been placed in a matrix that has us living out of fear. If we are faced with fearful thoughts we generally don't act out of love and compassion because of the clog in the artery of Divine love.

We are inundated with fear all through life, by design I might add. Most recently COVID-19. One good thing resulting from COVID-19 virus is the fact that people were forced to slow down, and reflect. It made me realize that we cannot trust the system to supply all of our needs. If there is a breakdown in the economic chain, an ugly side of humanity rears its ugly head. The toilet paper hoarders come out of the woodwork. Another looming fear is that of other countries as our enemies. The powers that be can always find a reason for war. Far too many folks are faced with the ongoing fear of making ends meet. Too many folks work more than one job and are finding it hard to still pay the rent. I began to realize the things that should be taught in school is how to purify water and how to grow food and how to cook and how to build and how to love. None of these things are taught in school.

As I stated before, part of the awakening is going through the dark night of the soul. Some of my friends admit that they have been going through this process. It is necessary for the progression of the soul. Me included. As I did my morning meditation, it was as though the Akashic Records were passing through my mind. I began to see all the things I had done that resulted in hurting people. Some of the things that flashed in my mind as I meditated were hard for me to face. However, I did it and continue to do it. I then say a prayer I learned from my eldest grandson. It goes this way, "I'm sorry please forgive me, thank you and I love you." I would hold a picture of the person that I may have harmed with my words or my behavior in my mind's eye, as I said the prayer. With that I would also forgive myself. Putting out that compassionate and loving energy to the universe is quite powerful for healing the world, and the collective energy that we share. They call the recording of our life the Akashic records. Many experiencers of near death say that when they experience the phenomena of near death that their lives pass before them.

The good the bad and the ugly. They report that they no longer fear death, and they end up leading more spiritually awakened lives.

So, the way to change the world is to change ourselves. Recognize the toxic thoughts that have helped to create this chaotic world. And that the chaos is a result of our incorrect thoughts. Those driven by fear rather than love. This love I am referring to can be defined as non judgement. According to near death experiencers there is no judgement upon death except for the fact that we judge ourselves. It's often times then that the person decides to reincarnate, to continue to teach and learn the lessons not yet learned in their previous lives. Remembering that there has to be negative on this particular dimension in order for us to manifest. Yin yang, duality, opposites. Recognize that our thoughts have been influenced by the powers that be by way of the media, school, religion etc. The school system has taught his story not history. There is never a full account of our history. The United States of America has many atrocities in our history that we are not held accountable for in history class. This country is presented as an exceptional country. The truth is not told in a way that would demand accountability.

One might say what is truth. Perhaps they say It's her story. I say truth is that which can be proved. People take offence when you challenge their faith. My beliefs have marginalized me from many family and friends. I think one of the biggest offences against the human mind is to believe things without evidence, and to continue through life with a closed mind.

Some of the things that occurred in my life are hard to believe and are deemed woo woo. And, for this reason I left them out of the book. I decided to include my experience while meditating on my picnic table in the sun while living in New Mexico. I had to include it because it is so relevant to the truth. The truth that god is the sun the light, and we are all part of god. And there is no god outside ourselves.

I explain in the book how I was enlightened while meditating on the idea that we are all part of god and god is the sun. The light. I had been reading a spiritual book that asked me to picture god as the sun in the middle of a wheel with spokes. The book went on to say that we are all somewhere on the wheel and that we are all connected and thus we are all one. I was trying to wrap my head around this idea because I was raised Catholic and consider myself a recovering Catholic. I say this because I was taught that we are all born with original sin, thus the guilt. I was taught that god was a man in the sky and he created us and we can't see him but we must have faith that he exists and we better behave or we could go to hell. In any case, I was trying to wrap my mind around the idea that god was the sun and we were part of god and all of a sudden, a million pin point light bulbs went off in my head. The lights were coming from the sun. This took place in my mind's eye to confirm the idea that god is the sun and we are all part of god.

Again, I am reminded that Carl Sagan said we are all made out of star stuff, the same elements. Once again, another hippy song nailed it. The Woodstock song, sung by Crosby Stills Nash and Young written by Joni Mitchell, "We are stardust we are golden we are billion-year-old carbon and we got to get ourselves back to the garden." Once again, the hippies nailed it. A pretty enlightened group.

I intend to prove through ontological mathematics that we are gods and part of the sun.

PREFACE

At the 11th hour of the 11th day of the 11th month, world war 1 ended and a mystery was begging to be solved.

Could the repeating 1's have a special value in the cosmic world? A value so important that the universe is using synchronicity to make that point. Einstein said that the language god wrote the universe in is math. Number in itself is math. There is a mathematical clue that applies to everyone. I discovered this clue in 2011, prior to the ending of the Mayan calendar.

In the year 2011 it was possible to take the last 2 digits of the year you were born and add it to the age you were in 2011, and the result will be 111 for everyone. It's a fact that many people who see 11 11 also see 111. Add that to the fact that we left the age of Pisces in 2011 and entered the age of Aquarius in 2012. Many people thought the ending of the Mayan calendar meant the ending of the world. It just meant the end of the age of Pisces and the beginning of the age of Aquarius.

The age of Aquarius is associated with the idea of peace and harmony. Could all these ideas be clues. Could the universe be trying to draw our attention to the symbolic meaning of all the 1's.

Could it be as simple as 1's symbolizing the power of our oneness. (united we stand divided we fall). Could the power of our collective focus and prayer taking place at one time on 11 11 at 11 am for 1 minute be instrumental in creating the critical mass needed to create a peaceful world?

Could the space between the 1's on each 11 be visually symbolic of a pathway. Are people seeing the 11's because it is time to choose a path.

Could it be that the universe is beckoning us to be united in our collective focus on peace and love. Is the universe giving us a very specific time to bring us all together in a collective effort with the intention of changing the current status quo of accepting war as the norm. Is 11 11 a time slot that we can use to unify.

More and more people are experiencing the 11 11 phenomena all the time. Are more and more people waking up to the idea that we have the power to make change? Is it time to jump aboard the love train? I say this because I believe that only love can turn this ship around. Let us use this time of 11 11 at 11 to unify our thoughts for 1 minute to focus on peace and love and our prayers will meet in the vast unseen spiritual internet and steer us in the direction of peace together.

CHAPTER 1

SYNCHRONICITIES

A spiritual awakening is occurring in human culture and is marked by coincidences. I first learned of this awakening when I read the Celestine Prophecies. It was not until the death of my son that I personally began to experience the coincidences. I now refer to the co-incidences as synchronicities.

This book is dedicated to my beloved son, whom I lost on **11/11/2002**. I have often heard it said that everything happens for a reason, and the loss of my son, and the paranormal experiences that have occurred since his crossing over have led me to believe that this is true. That is to say I am now a believer in the idea that there are no coincidences. My son's death sent me on a search, and my search led to a profound understanding of what the message of the **11 11** phenomena is trying to give us. The universe is addressing all of us by way of this phenomena. And I will explain exactly how the universe is speaking to all of us through synchronicities. I hope to introduce phenomena that will convince the reader that there is life after death and our loved ones can cross over to give us messages and to guide us if we are open to this idea.

The **11 11** phenomena is manifested by drawing the attention of the observer to **11:11** in many different ways. For example, one will look at the clock and see **11:11** numerous times throughout the day. Or, for example where ever there are numbers involved in a particular scenario that calls for one to look at numbers, an overwhelming number of times one would see 11s throughout the day, or at least too many times to be coincidence. The 11:11 phenomena has a very specific significance, which will become apparent as one reads on.

Sometimes people experience synchronicities in other ways. Some people see 3:33 or 4:44 or 5:55 etc. However, I think when people see repetitive numbers occurring, like 333 or 444, that there is a personal message for the observer in that synchronicity. At that point the experiencer often looks to numerology to find the meaning of that number and how it ties in to the message. It is the universe's way of pointing out that synchronicities have profound meaning, so pay attention to them and look for the meaning behind them. Many people call their number synchronicities an "angel minute." I think that all of this is true. I am sure all of the messages are personal and occur to help the observer evolve spiritually.

11:11 and **1:11** have particular meaning, and the meaning is a significant one and is meant for the world. It is meant to help us evolve collectively as one in an effort to change the world for the better.

In my case, since my son crossed over, he has reached into my dreams and entered into my consciousness in the most intelligent and creative ways. And, all in an effort to guide me.

There are many people out there who experience the 11:11 phenomena first hand, myself included. At first, I was not clear why I was seeing 11:11 too many times for me not to wonder why this synchronicity began occurring and continues to occur throughout the day every day of my life. I began to experience the phenomena shortly after my son died on 11:11.

Many folks experience the phenomena by association. By that I mean that there are folks that don't see 11 11 throughout their day, but they are drawn to look a 11 11 for certain reasons. For example, someone they know or love was born or died on that date and they are forced to look at the date simply because it marks the birth or death of someone they know and or love. Or some other event marked that date in their minds.

Many people experience synchronicities in various ways. For example, my daughter will be thinking of her brother that died, and all of a sudden, his favorite song will come on the radio station. She also experiences the 11:11 phenomena, along with my grandsons and 2 of my nephews. We all became observers of the 11 11 phenomena shortly after my son died on 11 11. And, of course there are people all over the world who see 11 11s throughout the day.

Another example is described to me by one of my friends. She and her daughter have been very close friends to me and my children. It was on 11:11, a couple of years after my son's death, that I got a call from this friend. She described to me how she was searching through some boxes of papers, when my sons picture fell out of the box she was rummaging through. Was it a coincidence? I don't think so and neither does she. My friend was one of those special people in my son's life who gave him love and provided ways for my son to express some of his skills. My son had issues but he was very bright, and talented as he was a good bass player and he enjoyed playing the guitar as well. She gave him jobs like putting in her kitchen ceiling fan. She provided ways for him to accomplish chores and shine. She and her daughter are also experiencers of the 11 11 phenomena as well.

CHAPTER 2

ABOUT MY SON

It's important for me to make clear at this time that my relationship with my son was anything but healthy. It was very painful to watch my son struggle through life as it seemed he was never really happy. He was one of those children that acted out often and did not do well in school and even had problems with his social life. Later on, in his life he got into hard drugs and experienced all the negative energy that life style brought to him and my entire family. My son was a troubled child, and difficult to raise but he was deeply loved by me, and his close family members, as well as some friends.

Raising my son was very difficult, and in a desperate attempt to find some guidance, and hoping for wisdom I took up meditation. I truly believe that meditation can open portals that allow for the spirit world to enter into our dreams and consciousness in the most intelligent and creative ways. However, wisdom does not come overnight.

My sons lack of social skills became more apparent when we were gathered in social settings. For example, when we would visit my cousin, whose son was born (co-incidentally) the exact same day as my son. He and my son both born 4/11 in 1979. But by comparison, my son and his cousin were exact opposites. My son did not seem to be as grounded or centered as his cousin or other children for that matter. My son had trouble making and keeping friends. My cousin's son was a happy little guy and my son not so much.

It was an interesting synchronicity that the same cousin who had a son the same day as mine, lost his brother (my cousin) on 11 11 in the 80's. The fact that my cousin died on 11 11 in the 80's didn't seem to have any meaning at the time. It wasn't until my son died that the synchronicities began to be apparent to me.

And oddly enough, I found myself at the university hospital on **11/11** in 2013 **11** years after my son's death, saying goodbye to this young man who was born the same day and year as my son. This young man lost his battle with his sudden health issues. These two young men born **4/11** died **11** years apart. And, I found it coincidental that I was wearing my veterans POW shirt, never forgotten. I always wear it on Veteran's Day. I never want to forget to honor the veterans who have given their life and limbs throughout history, fighting numerous wars. I'm bringing this up because **11/11** is also Veterans Day.

The fact that veteran's day takes place on 11 11 has a very important significance, which I will later explain. I believe that our attention is drawn to **11 11** to make an impression on us all as a human race. And, my son died at my mom's house where he lay on the floor beside his uncle, watching television. He never woke up and his body made an imprint on the carpet where he died. The imprint stayed there for years till there was a fire and the carpets were replaced. In fact, my nephew, who was very close to my son, would actually lay in the imprint to be close to my sons' spirit. My feeling is my son somehow knew that his death was supposed to call our attention to the importance of the **11 11** phenomena. His body made an impression and was symbolic of the importance of the **11 11 phenomena**. My son died of pneumonia, however, he also had in his system pain medications, so his respiratory system was further compromised by the drugs found in his system.

CHAPTER 3

THE FIRST INDICATION

I will never forget the day I received the call from my mom. She said, "Honey I have some bad news. Your son is gone." He had spent the night there at my mom's house. I told her why did he leave we had an appointment today and I was to pick him up at your house. She said no honey. He is gone, I can't wake him up, he is gone. I just remember screaming and throwing the phone. My daughter and I jumped in the car and raced to my mom's house. My immediate family began arriving at mom's as they heard the news of my son's death.

My next memory is sitting at mom's and my family slowly trickling in as they learned the news. We were sitting there waiting for the policeman to allow us to see my son's body. As we all sat at mom's trying to comfort one another, my dad looked at my mom and said to her, "Do you remember the television going off by itself early this morning?" Mom said, "Yes." Mom described how the television went on about 4 am, and it was up full blast and woke them up out of a sound sleep. Dad apparently had to get out of bed and go turn it off. As it turned out, the television went on full blast at the time that the coroner said my son died. I would say that that was the **first indication** that my son gave me that he had "broke on through to the other side." And that he was letting me know that he was using his energy to reach out to us.

There is a law of physics that states that energy cannot be created or destroyed, just change form. It became apparent to me that my sons' spirit (energy) didn't die. Only the vehicle, (his body) that he was experiencing this earth plane in had died. His spirit lives on, and he let me know that his spirit, which was pure energy now, had allowed him to turn that TV on and set it as loud as possible to let me know that he was still with me. And I have to tell you, the fact that that happened made his death a lot easier for me to handle emotionally. He knew I needed him to let me know that he was still with me.

CHAPTER 4

THE SECOND INDICATION

The funeral was of course, a sad affair. And, I remember standing in front of my son's casket along with other members of my immediate family, my mother being one of them. As we were standing around there, my oldest grandson blurted out, "Uncle smells!" My mother immediately put her hand over his mouth and said, "Shhhh!" I told my mom, "It's okay mom." His body does have a scent. It's how they embalm with the formaldehyde and then they cover it with the floral scent. You can't mistake it. After the funeral we all ended up over at my sisters to gather for food and conversation and family condolences.

I bring this up, because of what occurred later on after the funeral at my sister's where we all gathered to honor my son's memory. The same grandson who had mentioned the smell of my sons' body, came out of my sister's bedroom. He had been in the bedroom chatting with my sister's grandson as he lay on her bed with a stomach ache. He announced that it smells like uncle in there. I went in the bedroom to see what he was talking about. The smell of embalming fluid was strong in that room. I began picking up the coats of the people attending the gathering, thinking that maybe someone attending the funeral had brought that scent on their coat to my sister's house. My sister walked in when I was sniffing her husband's coat. She then related to me that her husband didn't even wear his coat in to the funeral.

The scent was so strong that we could all smell it and, her room then became the area that we all gathered in. It helped to ease the sorrow of my son's passing by knowing that he was not only there when my grandson made the statement about the odor, he followed us to sister's house to let us all know that energy never dies, just changes form. My son didn't die. His body did. He had merely changed form. He was now pure energy.

I can honestly say, knowing that his spirit lives on makes it so much easier to take the loss of a loved one. My son was never a very happy person through his struggles in life. I now knew he had reached that place where there is no more pain. I believe that his spirit reached that realm, or that frequency where only love exists. And, how blessed I am, that my son loved me enough to focus his energy in such ways that convinced me and started to convince the non-believers that there is indeed a spirit world. And, he could and did give us that message, that is to say that he let us know that his spirit was alive and well and yes he **broke on through to the other side.**

CHAPTER 5

THE THIRD INDICATION

The next scenario that I experienced with regard to my son's spirit letting me know that he was with me, occurred during my meditation shortly after his death. Not long after my son died, my daughter and I had moved to another home not far from the one we lived in at the time of my son's death. I was on the back-porch meditating, which had become a habit of mine. I began meditating 20 years earlier, in an effort to help me deal with what had become a struggle to raise my son, as it became apparent early on that my son had issues. Anyhow I was meditating in the sun, when in my mind's eye I saw the most beautiful cherub like lips I have ever seen. They floated there for a good minute or two. That may not seem like a long time, but considering that I have never been able to hold a picture in my mind's eye for more than a couple of seconds, I consider 2 minutes a long time.

Now and then I make a conscious effort to hold someone's form in my mind's eye. I do this when I am praying for that someone, and sending healing thoughts to them. I can only do it for a few seconds. I have never had a picture appear in my mind's eye without trying to make that picture appear to strengthen a prayer for example. So, I knew that my son's spirit was alive and well. And, in fact he was kissing me. And I should add at this point, that with each indication that my son gave me that his spirit was alive and with me came a feeling or a strong sense of the idea of forgiveness. That is to say, I knew he forgave me for not being the type of mother that raised a healthy happy boy. And, moreover, it gave me confirmation of the fact that he was no longer suffering and that he was in the light and in that place of love, light and energy because he was certainly able to use his energy to cross over to let me know he was in heaven and he was living in the light and under the umbrella of God's love.

I actually think that years of meditation increased my ability to tune into my son's vibrational frequency. I think meditation can remove veils that allow for these amazing paranormal events to occur.

CHAPTER 6

MATHEMATICAL CLUE THAT APPLIES TO ALL OF MANKIND

I read another book which gave me more insight regarding the 11 11s. The book describes how one of the Mayan temples called the Temple of the Descending Gods had some interesting symbols. I have never seen this Temple personally, but if it exists as the book indicated, then I must share the knowledge that I took from the symbols described in the book. The two **11**s in this Temple were symbolized by two pillars parallel to each other. Similar to two gates, or entryways, or pathways. The pictures surrounding one of the **11**s shows pictures of gloom and doom. People starving, skulls and bones etc... all the scary pictures that one would expect to find in a depiction of the worst-case scenario, with regard to world events. A reality based on a society guided by fear and hate. However, the other pillar represents the total opposite, where the crops are good and people are happy. The picture on this pillar brings forth a reality based on a society guided by love. Total opposite realities. I learned that we are here to evolve spiritually and learn to become love. As we go through life, we must remove ego. Once ego is removed then all there is, is love. All things negative stem from ego such as fear, hate, greed, envy ….

There are other ways that the **11:11** Phenomena draws the attention of the observer to the **11:11,** And, for those of you who are not experiencing the **11/11** phenomena in any of the ways I have described, I'm here to tell you that the universe, or god has designed a mathematical plan whereby every human being born, can relate to.

It was brought to my attention in the year 2011, the year prior to the ending of the Mayan calendar, that anyone who did this little **mathematical formula,** (so to speak) would come up with the same answers. In the year **2011**, it was possible to take the last 2 digits of the year in which you were born, and then add the age you will be in that year (in 2011). And the result will be **111** for everyone. For example, I was born in 1950. I take the last two numbers of my birth date, and add the 50 to age I was in 2011, and I was 61 years old. The two numbers add up to 111. Perhaps some people can remember when this was going around the Internet, and social media was ablaze with this little formula that rang true for everyone. **111** are another set of numbers experienced by observers of the phenomena.

I mentioned that many observers of the **11 11** phenomena also see **111.** Keep in mind the little mathematical formula which everyone can relate to, weather they are observers or not, since it rang true for everyone. And I believe that the missing **1**, is the part of the puzzle which involves free will. It is symbolic of the idea that we are all one (1). If we choose a path or gateway that is based on love for example, we will then complete the structure **(11)**. the missing **1,** that makes the number **11 (the gateway)** and the absence of the **1** is symbolic of the idea of free will and, once we consciously choose a path based on love, we then in essence are choosing a pathway that is symbolized by the **11**. The gateway to our collective reality. And it's our own free will that will determine the path we take. If we choose to live out of love then our path is clear and we will then be part of the collective that choose that path as well. Collectively we can create a reality based on the energy of love rather than the energy of fear. Conversely, if we choose a path based on fear, we will create that reality and our choice will complete the structure of the other gate. It is said that the two root emotions are **fear** and **love** and all other emotions stem from either of these two emotions. It seems clear to me that the Mayans understood this concept and were relating this information to people who are awake enough to catch on.

Maya means illusion. I think the Mayans understood the concept of how our thoughts create our reality and our collective thoughts create our collective reality. If we all had only loving thoughts, we could create a paradise or heaven on earth. By contrast our collective thoughts of fear have created our current experience. And its noteworthy to keep in mind that once fear or egoic thoughts are removed then all there is love. They are opposites. It seems there is a force or an agenda that wants us fearful. I am referring to the powers that be who design laws, and religious doctrines designed to perpetuate negative energy like wars and guilt, that keep us in fear. So, I can identify with the idea of illusion. Our collective experience on this planet is an illusion based on fear or incorrect thinking. That is to say if our collective thoughts stemmed from love then we could create a paradise. Once ego is removed, all there is, is love. So in conclusion our current experience is an illusion based on incorrect thinking. And as we begin to awaken, we can be active in getting rid of the illusion.

I do believe that the universe was addressing everyone on the planet at that point. Also, I'd like to point out that in the year **2011** we experienced four unusual dates. unusual dates, **1/1/11, 1/11/11, 11/1/11, 11/11/11**, These unusual occurrences happened just before the Mayan calendar ended. I'm just saying, or rather trying to point out that perhaps there is a reason for all these synchronicities. Perhaps these synchronicities are begging our attention. A wake-up call.

CHAPTER 7

VIBRATION AND FREQUENCY

It was Nikola Tesla who said that everything in life is energy, vibration and frequency. I learned in chemistry class that everything is made up of atoms and they are constantly vibrating with constant rapid random motion. Even though we can't see the motion, for example, we can't see the movement of fan blades as they are spinning to keep us cooled, because they are moving so fast. As humans we are also made up of atoms that are vibrating. And, everything has its own frequency at which it is vibrating. Each organ of the body has its own frequency at which it vibrates. Holistic healers and energy workers use particular oils that match the frequency of the organ to be addressed.

I read a book once that made the point that the spirit world occupies the same space as we do. We can't usually see them because they are vibrating on a different frequency. A good analogy is: If we are tuned in to a particular radio station, we are dialed into a particular frequency. All the other frequencies exist in the same space, but we have to tune into them to hear them. Same thing with the spirit world. They occupy the same space but they are vibrating at a different frequency than we are, so they are not visible. Unless at times their frequency crosses over to ours. They are referred to as apparitions, or ghosts. They are often fuzzy because the frequency may not be fully tuned in.

It was right after I read the book that said we occupy the same space as the spirit world that I was granted a wink and a nod from the universe. It happened in this way. I was in my barber shop located in the truck stop, watching the television, suddenly I heard a CB radio on my TV for a few seconds. Apparently, a driver's CB frequency crossed over to the frequency of my TV station. It was brief, but I got the message. The Universe gave me an affirmation regarding this idea. In other words, the universe was affirming the notion that frequencies do cross over. I call it a wink and a nod from the universe. I get these all the time. We probably all do, but since I know I pay attention.

The sound of music is a **vibration** that hits our ear. We can't see the sound waves, but the ear drum picks up the vibrational frequency of the sound waves and sends these vibrations to the brain where our brain translates (decodes them) into meaningful sounds such as words and language.

Mother earth has a frequency at which it vibrates as well. Native Americans referred to it as the heartbeat of mother earth. I learned that my ashram bowl (singing bowl) is tuned to 432 Hz. The Tibetan singing bowls are tuned to 432 Hz. And I learned that when the **OM** mantra is chanted, during meditation that the frequency of the vibration is said to be 432 Hz. This happens to be the vibrational frequency of everything natural in the universe.

Science has discovered the vibratory and oscillatory nature of the universe. They have discovered that there is a universal vibrational energy that all things in nature are in equilibrium with. These discoveries indicate the tuning standard of 440Hz are found to be out of sync, with this harmonious flow. It is believed that they have unhealthy effects on brain wave patterns. These effects could contribute to antisocial behavior, and our consciousness could be effected through dissonance, disharmony, and mathematical disunity. In 1932 a Nazi named

Joseph Goebbels was instrumental in changing the standard for tuning music from 432 Hz to 440 Hz. Could there be a conspiracy to keep people at a disadvantage with regard to achieving self-actualization and harmony and peace?

It is good to have an understanding of vibration and frequencies. As we speak words, we must remember that they have a vibration and frequency. It is the vocal chords that facilitate this action. As air passes over the vocal chords they create words based on the vibrating vocal chords. Thoughts have a vibration and frequency that is unheard by humans but the vibrations exist none the less. I have experienced this phenomena many times throughout my life. Often times I could feel someone staring at me even when they were behind me. I could just sense someone focusing on me. I felt the vibrations of their thoughts. And when I look back at them, they quickly turn away. In fact, I have gotten caught staring at someone, and I quickly turn away. It's rude to stare.

It is not unusual for people to say, "He has good vibes." These are not necessarily seen but felt. It's worth remembering to keep our thoughts pure and free of negative energy and to not speak angry words. I say this because words have a vibration as well as our thoughts. A wise doctor said, "be careful what you say, because your cells are listening." Not only are our cells listening to our words but our thoughts have a vibration too. If our thoughts are negative or of a low vibration, they can affect our health.

Everyone has their own frequency at which they vibrate. A healer will vibrate at a higher frequency as say a murderer. The genius, and inventor of alternate current, Nikola Tesla said the secrets to the universe have to do with energy, frequency, and vibration. Even music is measured by mathematical scales. And Einstein said the language god wrote the universe in was math. As an energy worker I do reflexology. It's interesting to note that every major organ in the body is represented by an area on the feet. And every organ has a different frequency at which it vibrates. And various essential oils address particular organs (represented on the feet) based on their common frequency at which they vibrate.

CHAPTER 8

CYMATICS

I saw a visual demonstration of how vibration and frequency effects matter. It is called **Cymatics.** In the demonstration, sand is scattered on a metal plate. A bow, like the one used to play a violin, is then scraped along the side of the metal plate to create a vibration. The sand responds to the vibration by forming patterns and the higher the frequency of the vibration, the more detailed the patterns become by forming breathtaking geometric patterns in perfect symmetry and absolute beauty. The higher the frequency the more complex and intricate the patterns become. These **patterns resemble sacred geometry**.

Sacred geometry is found and repeated throughout the universe. For example, the spiral shape of our **DNA**, the **shape of the galaxies**, the shape of a **sea shell**, the pattern of **petals in a sunflower.** Perfectly mathematically designed. There is something called the **golden ratio**, it is the mathematical value that is found throughout the universe and it points towards the idea that there are common factors that are shared throughout the universe. These sacred geometrical patterns that are found in nature are based on the **Fibonacci sequence**. And some people refer to these mathematical values that show up throughout the universe as the **fingerprint of god. Einstein** said the language that god wrote the universe in is math. The universal language, so is music, and it is based on mathematical scales. Proof of intelligent design.

This experiment can be done with water too. Amazing patterns formed by frequencies. The extraordinary life works of Dr. Massaru Emoto is documented in his book, "The Hidden Messages in Water." In his book he demonstrates how water exposed to loving and benevolent and compassionate human words, intentions, thoughts, and sounds transforms the molecular structure of water. The results are very aesthetically pleasing molecular formations in the water molecules.

On the other hand, water that is exposed to fearful and discordant human intention resulted in disconnected, disfigured shapes.

The Cymatics demonstration made it visibly clear to me how vibration and frequency was able to shape the sand into geometric shapes based on frequency. And, Dr. Emoto's experiments with water taught me that the frequency of the vibrations of our thoughts and intentions can effect the shape of water.

As I continued researching into this amazing phenomenon, I found that the current standard for tuning instruments in the western world is 440 Hz. However, in other parts of the world the standard for tuning instruments is 432 Hz, which is the same as the vibration of the heart- beat of mother earth. In other words, we commonly tune our instruments to a frequency that does not resonate with the sacred frequencies that produce sacred geometry and are referred to by some as the **god frequency**.

Our modern-day musical scale is out of sync when compared with the original Solfeggio scale. It might be beneficial to replace the dissonant western scale, with the original Solfeggio scale, in an effort to relax and allow us to vibrate at a frequency that resonates with peace. I try to spend time listening to Oriental flute music as well as Native American flute, because I have been told that these types of music incorporate the 432 scale. I notice that my clients relax quicker when Oriental flute and Native flute music is played while I am giving therapeutic massage. I love it when the client gives off that relaxing breath that I hear them take when they are fully in the zone.

I am a big fan of a lot of rock music that is from the 60s, 70s, and 80s. Many of those songs give off good vibrations and touch my heart too. I am reminded that even the sounds of words have a vibration and frequency. The words of many of the songs of the '60s resonate with me. Particularly ones that are passionate about social justice and anti-war music. And, pro-peace and love songs. Music can be a tool to raise human nature and connect us with source. Or, music can be used to create disharmony and anxiety. Certain rap songs I find cause disharmony, at least that is the case for me.

I learned that the Rothschilds through their agents in the Rockefeller family, joined the American Federation of Musicians and convinced the group to endorse a standard of 440 Hz tuning for all orchestras and concert performing musicians. These folks are often associated with hidden agendas, that do not benefit mankind.

I also learned that a Nazi war criminal who served under Hitler as minister of propaganda set the standard for the western world. And he used the dissonant western scale to produce disharmony and anxiety. If this is true, then it would seem like perhaps there is a conspiracy to keep people at a disadvantage in their search for peace. Could it be that the powers that be often referred to as the deep state, or the secret societies or those with a hidden agenda are trying to promote discontent on a mass level. Could it be that there is a hidden agenda that wants to influence our energy in a negative way? If so, then it would seem that they somehow benefit by the negative energy they have made standard because it is beneficial to them.

It is good to have an understanding of vibration and frequencies, so that we understand how important positive thoughts are to our mental and physical health. It's important to have *good, good, good vibrations* (Another song popularized in 1966). It makes sense to keep our thought forms free of negative energy, since we are 75% water, and if our thoughts can change the shape of water as I mentioned, then imagine what our thoughts do to the water within us. Too much negativity can affect us since we are mostly water. Our thoughts have a profound impact on our health. Words can have an impact on our health as well. A wise and famous doctor said be careful what you say, because your cells are listening.

CHAPTER 9

EMBRACED BY THE LIGHT

I once read a book that I found very interesting. This particular book is part of the reason I think that my son may have known that his death was supposed to call our attention to the 11 11 phenomena. The person writing the book describes how she had a near death experience. The author describes how she went to the light and met Jesus and the angels. She was overcome with the most intense indescribable, unconditional love. The angels replayed her life before her and showed her all the good things she had done in her lifetime and what a huge impact that her good deeds had on the world, like a ripple effect, and all the angels rejoiced with her. Then they replayed her life for her and showed her all the deeds she had done that had impacted the world in a negative way, like a ripple effect. The surprising thing was that there was **no judgement**. There was only deep sorrow shared by her and the angels. Deep sorrow for how her deeds had affected humanity in a negative way.

The angels explained that we should never judge one another. They explained that even a homeless person or a bum should not be judged or looked down upon, or anybody for that matter, because they could have chosen to come back to earth to teach and learn lessons. And they are perhaps very brave souls who chose to return knowing life would be very difficult. For example, if one feels sorry for being greedy on this earth plane, they may choose to come back to earth school to experience poverty. Or perhaps they come back as a bum to test others' behavior towards the less privileged.

In the book the angels explained that we are here on this earth plane to learn to love one another. To realize we are all connected and that we are all One. I learned that we are here to evolve spiritually and learn to become love. As we go through life, we must remove ego. Once ego is removed then all there is, is love. All things negative stem from ego such as fear, hate, greed, envy....

As we evolve spiritually, we become more loving. The angels explain that earth school is about learning and teaching. They explained that we are both teachers and students on this planet. My thoughts are that my son perhaps chose to come to earth, in an effort to impress upon me and others the importance of 11 11, as it marked his death, and called my attention to the date. On a personal level it taught me that all my son was lacking was love. Whatever the question, love is the answer. I did not give him good love. I was too busy tap dancing to the fear of not having enough money to make ends meet. Often times I was working 2 and sometimes 3 jobs which left little time or energy to focus on my son's need for my positive attention.

In the book the author describes heaven or being in the light in such incredible ways. The wonderful feeling of being totally loved when in the presence of these beings. The feeling was so awesome that she didn't want to come back. But she does and I learned from her near-death experience that we come to earth to teach and learn. So perhaps my son came to earth to live and die to give an important message to me and I feel it necessary to share with the world. I think his death was meant to make an impression. To impress upon me the importance of the **11 11** phenomena and how we can impact the world as **one** to make changes for the better. Not only does my son's life and death play into this scenario or intelligent design. It seems to me that we all play into this scenario, we are all part of the design.

CHAPTER 10

RAISED CATHOLIC

I was so intrigued by the idea of **no judgement**, because of how I was raised as a Catholic. We were taught that we were born with original sin. I was taught to fear god. I was taught to believe that when we die, we go to hell, if we are bad. Yet, I have heard that Jesus made the point numerous times not to be afraid. The words **fear not** are repeated by Jesus numerous times. It got me to wonder why many religions, with all the years of doctrine and wisdom would use **fear** to gain obedience, unless the energy of fear was somehow useful to them then and now.

In catholic school we were routinely obliged to confess our sins. My stomach would be tied into knots as my turn to confess my sins to the priest was approaching. We were also obliged to go to church before school during the month of May. Church was just a block from school, so it was convenient for our class to walk to school after mass was over. I was so afraid of confession, to the point that one time, while waiting in the line to confess my sins, I faked being sick to avoid the confessional. In truth my sins went something like this when I was in the confessional, and not faking illness.I would say to the priest on the other side of the little sliding window, "Bless me Father for I have sinned. My last confession was last week. These are my sins: I lied to my mom, I sassed my mom and dad and I disobeyed them." The priest responded by telling me to say 5 Hail Marys and 10 Our Fathers. Whew. Ok I can live with that. I can say 15 prayers.

My fear came in part from my classmate's experience. She was ahead of me in line to confess her sins. While she was in the confessional box confessing her sins to the priest, he blurted out **"you did what"**. Everyone in the church heard him. The poor girl came out of the confessional literally shrinking within herself from embarrassment. Thank god it wasn't me who father screamed at. I have often wondered what a 7-year-old child could have done to prompt the priest to embarrass her in that manner.

I learned in catholic school that I don't want to die with sins on my soul. If I die with a mortal sin then I will go to hell and burn forever. I learned that if I die with a menial sin then I will just go to purgatory, and I will burn for a while. I also was taught that we are all born with original sin. According to them we all start of bad. Talk about using fear to gain obedience, that's the best example I can think of. I now refer to myself as a recovering catholic. By that I mean that I have eliminated the guilt of having been born with sin as I was led to believe.

My experiences have led me to theorize that those of us who see the 11:11 more than coincidence would allow, are those of us who are at least in our minds questioning conventional religion and have an open mind to the idea that there's something else and it's called spirituality. Or, those of us who are vibrating on a particular frequency that resonates with truth. I would like to say that there are religious people that are extremely spiritual. I know them. I've met them. Some are in my extended family. I have to say that those who are spiritual and call themselves Christians do embody the true meaning of Christianity. That is to say they are kind, compassionate and tolerant and loving. I have some family members who are extremely religious and spiritual and benevolent. And I have been blessed with their benevolence. Particularly when my son died, many people were very helpful by donating money for funeral expenses etc…

Although I'm not religious, and I take issue with religions that promote war and endorse those doctrines that place women as second class. However, I do honor those religions that demonstrate great love. Including the more pagan religions like Native American spirituality where everything was sacred. For God is pure Love, and Jesus was sent here to demonstrate what great love can do. Jesus' love and light are introduced in the new testament. He taught us love and forgiveness. And I believe that Jesus vibrated on such a frequency that he could walk on water. I do pick and choose those parts of the religious doctrines that I think shed light and wisdom and allow me to understand the 11/11 phenomena. I do pick and choose parts of various religious teachings when they resonate with me and the idea of love, and when these teachings support the position that I assume throughout this book.

CHAPTER 11

FORGIVENESS IS DIVINE

It should come as no surprise that judgement should **not** be a part of the fabric of many religious doctrines. The biggest statement that Jesus made with regard to his suffering and death is the idea of forgiveness. **"Forgive them father for they know not what they do."** After being tortured he forgave his tormentors. I don't think that the idea and importance of forgiveness can be down played. I think that the success of Alcoholics Anonymous or Drug Addicts Anonymous is because an important step in recovery is that one must forgive one's self for all the sins they commit, particularly where drugs and alcohol are concerned. And the sins against loved ones in particular are often times numerous, where drugs and alcohol are concerned. That is why making amends is so important for recovery. Once forgiveness of oneself can be achieved, one can then forgive others. That is to say, we are more tolerant of others and their sins when we have forgiven ourselves. **Forgiveness is divine**. And, I have heard that Jesus died for our sins, that we be forgiven. So, I ask those who judge others, who are we to override Jesus. He has already forgiven us.

My personal experience as an energy worker and reiki practitioner is that the more that I forgive myself for all of the sins I have committed against others, and the less I judge others the stronger my craft becomes. The more I forgive others, and the less I judge others, the more effective my energy work becomes. In other words, the more I live out of love the stronger my medicine becomes. If we hold anger and do not practice forgiveness then the anger is like a clog in the arterial line of the Divine energy of god and love. I have heard it said that "**Love** is the absence of **judgement**." I have also heard that **love** is the opposite of **fear**.

I believe the spiritual concept that embraces the idea that everyone is as good as they possibly can be at any particular point in time in their lives. It is what it is, so we must deal with it in the most loving and compassionate way possible. Whatever the question Love is the answer. People don't plan their whole lives from childhood to be bad. We were not born bad as the catholic religion taught us in catholic school. As I said before it was referred to as original sin.

Our environment has a lot to do with how we behave. People that are prone to misbehave are pretty much unable to behave differently. I believe when one misbehaves it is because somewhere along the line, they are lacking love. And when raising children love takes on the form of guidance through example. Also, time spent with focus and interest on the child. I realized that somewhere along the line that I dropped the ball where my son was concerned.

We are here to evolve spiritually, often times people don't know how to act in a more acceptable way. They really don't know better, or they are unable to control themselves. They know not what they do nor do they know the impact it has on humanity. And even if they did understand that concept, it does not guarantee that they can control their behavior. Our judicial system is heavy on punishment and lacking success in rehabilitation. Those that are hardest to love need love the most.

I once read a story about a tribe of people living in Africa. The story described how they deal with people that misbehave. All activity stops in this village. The misbehaving person, is placed in the center of a circle that is formed by all the people in the village. Then everyone takes a turn at addressing this person in the circle. Each person takes a turn at saying something good about the person in the circle. There is no punishment, there is only reassurance that that person in the circle is loved and worthy of being loved. This method is very effective in addressing negative behavior. It's better than putting a guy in a cage. I can't imagine being caged. Especially if the crime has no violence associated with it.

Jesus said **"forgive them father, for they know not what they do."** Yet, many folks think they are doing the right thing when they judge people. And why wouldn't they, as many religions promote judgment and fear. And in their blindness, and desire to please god, they follow various religious doctrine in an effort to be good Christians, Jews, Muslims etc. And let's face it religious doctrines have allowed for the most horrific punishments to be meted out throughout history. One example is the inquisition. The catholic church established a tribunal called the inquisition to try persons accused of being a heretic, that is, of revolting against religious authority. My understanding is that technology was involved in actually figuring out the best ways to prolong torture, without killing too quickly the person being tortured. I once saw a sticker that resonated with me, it read "When religion ruled the world, they called it the Dark Ages." Let that one sink in.

Today we still see people being beheaded and stoned to death, in the name of god. The super max prisons, where human contact is at a minimum is a form of mental torture. And I think electrocution is a form of torture too. I recently heard of a man being executed in a southern state, by lethal injection. The observer describing the execution said it was obvious that the man suffered as he writhed in pain for a full 35 minutes. I have known several folks that have overdosed on heroin and ended up dead. It amazes me that a lethal dose of an opiate such as heroin cannot be used as a method of execution. I know it works. I know several people who have died in that manner. No pain, just lights out.

Does it not make sense since Jesus died for our sins and the biggest demonstration of his torturous death was the fact that he forgave his tormentors. It is not easy to forgive people when they hurt us, that is why forgiveness is divine. Often times we need the help of god or our higher self to overcome anger and forgive others that have hurt us. If we don't apply forgiveness to our lives then we have a clog in the artery of the divine energy. Just like when we have a clog in our arteries, blood can't flow through readily. If we hold anger and resentment then the divine energy is unable to flow through us.

I think that is why the 12-step program is successful for so many. It requires very serious steps that lead to spirituality. Another successful program to combat addiction is **vision quest**. It involves getting in touch with nature by being out in the natural world alone. Very much along the lines of Native Americans stepping into manhood.

It wasn't until the death of my son, that I needed to apply the spiritual knowledge which would save me from the depths of depression that guilt can throw a soul in. At least if I needed forgiveness for speaking hurtful words, I could apologize as long as the person was alive. I am very good at apologizing if I offend someone. I am a firm believer in the idea I don't have to be right I have to be happy. And a sincere apology goes a long way when dealing with people whom I have offended.

Once someone has crossed over like my son did, you can't tell them that you are sorry or that you love them. I desperately needed to tell my son that I am sorry for not raising him to be happy and mentally healthy. However, his spirit would not let me feel guilt. He let me know that I must not feel guilty and I must not be overcome with depression. Every time my mind wanted to think about all the things, I did wrong, I would instantly be inundated with the things that I did right. I know he is responsible for allowing those good thoughts to overshadow the negative ones.

As I stated before, my journey led me to many sources of information especially on the spiritual level. I was introduced to a book called "A Course in Miracles." by my very first metaphysical teacher. She was well versed on the spiritual concepts put forth in the book and the concept of the new age thought regarding spirituality. She and her husband were very good friends of mine. Their daughter was my son's first real girlfriend.

My friend saw me struggling with my son. She tried to set me on the right path with the Book called " A Course in miracles." However, I was not ready to apply the knowledge that I would have gained had I been able to relate to the very sacred knowledge that the book teaches. The information did not resonate with me yet or I was not vibrating on the level required to receive the message within the book. I had not suffered enough yet. I once read that suffering actually brings us to seek god, because if we don't suffer, we might get to thinking who needs god. We are all broken, in some way, but the cracks of being broken is how the light gets in. The course emphasizes forgiveness. And it makes sense because I have heard it said numerous times that forgiveness is divine. And, I believe forgiveness of oneself is paramount for spiritual progression. Once one forgives themselves, they can then forgive others and the application of forgiveness mandates the removal of judgment. So, we must resist that urge to judge others. In conclusion I believe that religion is believing in someone else's experience, and spirituality is believing in our own experience.

CHAPTER 12

QUANTUM PHYSICS

The type of scientists that deals with atoms and subatomic particles are called physicists. I have to explain as much as I can understand about this subject. A good bit of what I am going to get into relates to it. I was led to watch a documentary film that made a strong case for the idea that our thoughts create our reality. This movie, involves an experiment. In the experiment an electron microscope is used to show how thoughts effect matter. The demonstration showed how a droplet of water formed into beautiful white snowflake-like patterns whenever the water was being focused on with loving thoughts by monks. The water droplet formed a beautiful intricate pattern. And then people were asked to focus on the water with hateful thoughts and the water turned into a very uneven, unattractive shapes of black and orange.

This experiment strongly suggests that our thoughts effect matter. And moreover, our collective thoughts are even more powerful. One of my favorite spiritual teachers is famous for this quote, "Be careful what you say, (words are vibration) your cells are listening." I would add be careful what you think as well. And remember we are mostly made up of water. Like 80% or higher. If our thoughts can affect water by turning it into beautiful shapes, just think of what our negative thoughts can do to us, since we are mostly water. Our thoughts have energy, because science says everything is energy.

Einstein is quoted as saying **"Everything is energy and that's all there is.** Our thoughts are waves of energy vibrating at a particular frequency. Often times people can read a person's vibrations. We always want to be around someone with good vibrations. I have had the experience in school of someone staring at me. I couldn't see it but I just knew, and I would turn around and sure enough they were staring at me. I guess I was feeling the vibrational energy of their thoughts.

The visual in the movie was helpful in driving home the idea that our thoughts do create our reality or they influence matter. I began to relate it to the idea that our collective thoughts create our collective reality. I was then reminded about a Mayan temple called The Temple of the Descending God, and how the two realities were manifested by the drawings around each 11. It became apparent that it's better that collectively we have loving thoughts and acts if we want to influence the world in a positive way.

New Age Religion suggests that if we all only held thoughts of love that we would create a paradise collectively, since our thoughts create our reality and our collective thoughts create our shared experience here on this earth plane. It sounds reasonable to believe we could actually manifest this reality. Imagine all the people living life as One. We are all part of this collective consciousness. Ghandi and Einstein both said that if 2% of the world's population focused on peace at the same time that we could change the world into a more peaceful existence. Collectively we could bring about a paradise. We are to the universe as a wave is to the ocean. We are part of the whole.

CHAPTER 13

SACRIFICING ON TOP OF THE PYRAMIDS

I have heard that the **Mayan Indians** performed sacrifice on top of the pyramids. It is said that they sacrificed to please the gods. I have read that there is indication that the Mayan Indians saw these (gods) beings descend from the sky. Who were these gods? I'm wondering if they are the same gods that instructed them to build these unbelievable pyramid shaped rock structures. No one can figure out to this day how these structures were built, with so much precision. I have also heard it said that the Mayan Indians sacrificed to please the gods. I think they were instructed how to build these elaborate structures just for the drama of this monumental act of sacrifice done before the entire population to view. This must have caused great fear.

It isn't a quantum leap to think that these visitors that descended from the sky helped build these amazing structures as well as huge astronomical towers used to chart the stars. I have to ask why would beings capable of flight from other worlds, demand such a horrific act that would instill such fear in the natives. I'm wondering if these beings fed off of the fearful energy that had to permeate the landscape. It had to be a frightening sight.

There is plenty of artwork carved in stone. Lots of scary monster faces carved in so many places in Mexico and South

America. The Mayans sacrificed to please the gods. These acts of sacrifice created fear so strong the monsters could feed on it all year long.

CHAPTER 14

THE DISAPPEARANCE OF THE MAYANS

I have often wondered about the disappearance of **the Mayan Indians**. There is indication that the cities were abandoned. It's not like they packed their belongings and moved on. It's more like they just vanished and left their belongings there. I have often wondered, perhaps the Mayans began to question the status quo at some point. I wonder if at some point they were tired of the fear they must have experienced from the ceremonial like sacrifice. I wonder if on a collective level they were praying and reached a critical mass and changed their reality by vibrating collectively to another dimension. Our thoughts have energy and they create our reality. Perhaps their collective thoughts changed their reality. In other words, they vibrated out of there. Perhaps they reached a critical mass. That number needed to create a change. Perhaps the collectively vibrated to another dimension.

One example of collective thoughts creating a desired reality is **sun dance**. Native Americans danced to the beat of the drum for a reason. They understood that their focused collective thoughts could in fact bring sun. And rain dance could bring the reality of rain. This may seem like a crazy idea, but I can assure you that myself and my grandsons do this regularly. Often times on my numerous walks with the grandsons, we would embark on bringing out the sun. And I can't really remember a time when the sun did not respond to our meditation and focus on bringing it out. Even if only briefly. However just enough to let us know that we connected with the light, we then acquiesce to the idea that the rain is needed.

CHAPTER 15

ANOTHER CLUE

The Celestine prophesies is another book that my journey led me to. The book is based on ancient manuscripts that were found in Peru. These manuscripts were apparently left by the Mayan natives and found by the Incas. The manuscripts revealed certain insights. The first insight is that a new spiritual awakening is occurring in human culture, and the awakening is brought about by a critical mass of individuals who experience their lives as a spiritual unfolding, a journey in which we are led forward by mysterious coincidences. (Synchronicities). And of course, one synchronicity that is being experienced on a collective level is the 11 11 phenomena.

It is no co-incidence that my path led me to the people who became my spiritual teachers, and they gave me more insight with regard to living in peace, which was to become a daunting task with regard to what the future was to bring me. The death of my son was devastating. The elimination of fear in our lives is a factor in achieving peace. And fear is the opposite of love. I think that I lived in fear so much of my life as I look back on how I could have made better choices in my life. And I realize how fear affected my decision making. The fear of not having the means to feed my family became a diving force in my life. I worked way too much, in an effort to provide for my son and myself. And when there was a reprieve for work, my time was not devoted to my son as it should have been. I was selfish with my time. I later learned how effective massage therapy could have been to my son's health. We store emotions in our cells and massage is a great way to releasing painful emotions. My son was a hurting unit because he wasn't my priority. If only my love for my son were not overshadowed by fearful thoughts of not having enough money to provide, then perhaps my son would have been happy and healthy.

So fearful thoughts dominated my behavior as well as selfishness on my part, which is also a result of fear. Fear and love are the two emotions that bring about our experiences. Our realities are actually based on our thoughts, which drive our behavior.

Our thoughts and emotions have a vibration, and a frequency that cannot be heard by humans, but they can gather momentum so to speak as they gather energy when other peoples' thoughts and emotions resonate with them. For example, when people are on the same page with their intention to bring about a healing or a more peaceful world. Like in the case of collective meditation or prayer.

That is why prayer circles can be so powerful, when those involved have the same intention. Einstein and Ghandi both said if 2% of the world's population were to focus with intention on bringing about a peaceful world, that we could change the world. It would involve bringing about a critical mass of people meditating (praying) at the same time. The time and date of 11 11 might increase the strength of the intention because of the relevance. Perhaps the universe is trying to impress upon us that the time of 11 11, or the date, can be a powerful symbolic number in helping us be unified in our attempt to change our reality to one of peace and love as we were promised. A paradise.

Perhaps we could create heaven on earth. The fact that in 2011 there were 4 unusual dates to once again impress upon us the importance of oneness and having a specific time with which to unify us. I do believe that the universe was once again addressing everyone on the planet at that point. In the year **2011** we experienced four unusual dates. **1/1/11, 1/11/11, 11/1/11, 11/11/11,** These unusual occurrences happened just before the Mayan calendar ended. I'm just saying, or rather trying to point out that perhaps there is a reason for all these synchronicities. Perhaps these synchronicities are begging our attention. I think that these times give us a framework whereby we can all unify to increase our collective thoughts of love for each other and mother earth and change our collective reality. **A Wake-up call** that we should all heed on these particular dates and times that will bring our thoughts and intentions together as one and be enhanced by the symbolism of 1s (ones) that the universe is pointing out.

Perhaps we could create a world where finances and material constructs, do not take precedence over our health and the health and well-being of our children, as well as the health of the earth the air the water and the food. Right now, for many folks, the failing economy takes precedence over the health of the general public. The corona virus is raging on as I write this. Many folks are taking to the streets to express their desire to go back to work to assume their lifestyle of working. Many are afraid of losing all the material things that they have acquired. Many are faced with not being able to pay rent or their mortgage, because they can't work, many people are afraid to lower their level of comfort as they are draining their savings. On some level everyone is forced to evaluate our ways of living. The pandemic has affected us all in some way. Panic sets in and the fear makes people hoard. Hoarding is self-centered and excludes the idea of oneness.

This virus is magnifying the choices people make. And some folks are realizing that we can't eat money. It is bringing to light how far off the track we have drifted on a collective level. It's more obvious how sick our society has become. It is no measure of health to be well adjusted to a sick society. And, our moral compass is more visible now that we have these challenges facing us on a global scale. The immorality of our capitalistic society is magnified as we see people hoarding and demanding to go back to work out of fear, even if it means endangering the health and well-being of our loved ones, as well as others. A light has been cast on just how harmful capitalism can be when we are faced with the choices that this virus is leading us to make. It is becoming easier to recognize those who live out of love as opposed to those who live out of fear.

I do believe that the people who are experiencing the awakening code are vibrating at a certain frequency whereby they are receiving the universal message first hand. And then there are those who are guided to look at the date of 11 11, because it marks some event, like a birthday or some other important event. Since Veterans Day takes place on 11 11, that day draws many people to pay attention to that date. And it is a synchronicity that the universe chooses this date to draw people's attention to. November 11th because it marks the end of **WAR.** In fact, it marks the end of WWI.

Perhaps we should take more seriously 111 that we are all forced to look at because of the mathematical clue that was given us regarding our birthdates. We should consider that the universe is giving us a clue that we should all make a collective effort to **END** all **WARS.** Nothing produces more fear than war. Our veterans and soldiers and those who experience war first hand can validate that statement. I am reminded of the words of another song. The words were **WAR WHAT IS IT GOOD FOR. ABSOLUTELY NOTHING!!!**

Einstein said that the language God wrote the universe in was math. Thus, the mathematical clue given to all by god or the universe. I also believe that music is a universal language. And I want to remind people that math is based on mathematical scales too.

CHAPTER 16

MAYANS WERE USHERING US IN

Many people thought that the ending of the Mayan calendar signified the end of the world. However, I have come to believe that the clues indicate rather an end to the age of pieces and an ushering in of the Age of Aquarius. The Mayans were brilliant. I remember hearing a song about them. It went "A thousand years ago the Mayans predicted every solstice equinox and moon eclipsis." These natives had pyramids. They charted the moon and the stars. It was then that I realized 5 things occurred at the same time. At **12/21/2012**.

Number 1. The age of Aquarius began
Number 2. The age of Pieces ended
Number 3. There was a galactic alignment
Number 4. The Mayan calendar ended
Number 5. The winter Solstice began at exactly 11
            11 Greenwich mean time

I believe the occurrences were synchronistical in as much as the age of Aquarius as well as all of the 5 synchronicities I described above occurred at exactly **11 11 am** on December 21st, 2012 Greenwich mean time zone. However, where I live in Colorado, all this occurred at **4:11** am in my time zone. And of course, it made me think of my son and his cousin, both were born on 4/11. It dawned on me **we** were **beginning** a new era called the age of Aquarius. Just as my son and his cousin started a beginning, a new physical existence here on earth. Both born on **4 11**, born the same day but both total opposite little guys in their behavior. It remined me of **fear** and **love** being total opposites. One little guy was raised by a mother whose life was shadowed by fear. And one little guy whose was raised by parents whose lives were not overshadowed by fear. It's hard to not factor in all these synchronicities including the fact that both of these young men died **11** years apart.

I have to say that the song that I remember from the late 60's or early 70's called Aquarius, by Fifth Dimension, has bolstered my opinion with regard to our collective ability to bring about a reality based on love. The group called the **Fifth Dimension,** sang their hearts out with words like Harmony and understanding, sympathy, and trust abounding. I believe that since the age of Aquarius is here now, and we are waking up to the idea that we have a choice to create a reality based on love since we are in the age of **Aquarius.** That's the reality I'm talking about.

The song **"Aquarius"** was released in 1969. I think the words are more relevant than ever. I will repeat some of the lines to the song and how they are still relevant today.

> **When the moon is in the seventh house**
> **And Jupiter aligns with Mars**
> **Then peace will guide the planet**
> **And love will steer the stars**
> **No more falsehoods or derisions**
> **Mystic crystal revelations'**
> **And the minds true liberation**

CHAPTER 17

NO MORE FALSEHOODS OR DERISIONS

The second line of the song refers to the galactic alignment that took place. Line 3 and 4 refer to the paradise we could create with our collective intentions and thoughts.

This 5th line on the song resonates with me in as much as it means that there will be no more contemptuous ridicule or mockery by those who I would describe as Sheeple, not people. By that I mean the folks that would call the ideas I am presenting as crazy or consider it woo woo. And I don't blame these folks. We have been so conditioned to accept things as they are as normal. Since I have awakened enough to question the status quo I have been called crazy along with other names. I do think out of the box and when you do this you are ridiculed. If you question religion, or war or any of the things that we have been taught to swallow or believe are a necessary part of life, then you are going against the grain of society. I do believe as time goes on and people wake up and add to the collective, those of us who think differently will not be mocked or ridiculed or called crazy anymore. Thus, the words to the song make sense to me. **No more falsehoods or derisions** relates to the fact that we are (the human race) is beginning to wake up and the veils are continuing to be removed to uncover the truth. The last line refers to that idea of waking up. The last line makes sense to me. **"And the minds true liberation, Aquarius."** We are waking up.

And this song truly resonates with me on several levels, the words **mystic crystal revelation** for example. I was introduced to crystal healing power a few years back. This is how the scenario occurred. I had been very ill with chronic pain. I wasn't sure if it was my teeth, my ears, my sinuses, my head, but I suffered from lack of energy and I had big dark circles under my eyes. The worst part was lack of energy. I had been to the doctor and finished a couple courses of antibiotics and I couldn't shake the illness. Anyhow, I was in the habit of meditating, but this particular morning I decided to use my crystals in my meditation. So, I began meditating with all my crystals around me and in my hands and got in my zone by using my mantra of **ommmm.** Within minutes I heard crackling in my head and began draining and spitting out infection. I was so grateful to find some relief. The words **mystic crystal revelation** took on a new meaning for me. It was then that crystal magic was revealed to me.

It was not until later that I understood how crystals work. One day a strange man wondered into my hair cutting shop. He began talking to me about crystals out of nowhere as if he knew me. He began explaining to me about crystals. He told me that crystals are used in computers. He said that they are also used in microphones.

He explained to me that crystals are in microphones because they pick up the vibration of your vocal chords and copy your vibrations, so they are instrumental in picking up the vibration of your voice so that the sound imitates the voice so it can be heard over the microphone. Or that's how I understood it. So, I figured that the crystals I used in my meditation picked up my vibrations as a healer as I verbally vibrated with the mantra of **ommmmm.** And my healing powers were enhanced by the crystals I held. I then began using them in my healing repertoire.

CHAPTER 18

THE IDEA OF ONENESS

So far, I have established the idea of fear versus love as demonstrated by the two pathways represented by the two pillars in the temple of the descending gods. Also, the idea of Oneness represented 4 times by the two 11's. In other words, there are four ones in 11 11, this emphasizes the idea of us being one, by mere virtue of the repeated ones. I mentioned that many observers of the **11 11** phenomena also see **111**, and I explained its significance with regard to free will, and the fact that the universe is calling everyone's attention to the fact that 111 relates to all of us by way of the mathematical formula that I explained.

In order to fully understand this idea of oneness, I must introduce the idea of the universal mind. Or put another way universal consciousness or our collective consciousness. I read a book once, in the book the author described the hundred monkey syndrome. He explains that scientists working with monkeys, on various islands, realized that when a certain concept or idea was learned by the hundredth monkey, that all the monkeys on the islands then knew that concept at that point. And that is called **critical mass.** In other words, critical mass was reached at the point that the hundredth monkey learned that concept being taught. And the whole idea of the hundredth monkey syndrome points to the idea that there is a collective pool of knowledge or consciousness that monkeys tap into in the monkey metaphysical world. Another example may be cows turning in unison. Fish act in unison as well.

Humans have the ability to tap into the collective consciousness that apparently exists where humans are concerned as well. Just another expression of our oneness on some level unseen. We are consistently interacting with this pool of consciousness. I believe that this is the very same pool of consciousness that allows **the diviner (those individuals who can use the divining rods to find water)** the ability to tap into that pool of consciousness that is available to all of us.

Some people are better at tapping into universal mind or universal knowledge, than others, but I think we are all capable of it. And using the pendulum is another tool to tap into the pool of our collective knowledge that knows all things. I guess you could say tapping into that part of our consciousness where god individualizes in all of us. Since the temple of god dwells within (within all of us). That is why I meditate. I go within to that point of consciousness where god individualizes in in me as he does in all of us. It is the higher self. That is where the term **namaste** comes from. This is a popular term that is often used by those spiritual new age hippy types, and others who believe that the temple of god dwells within. It comes from the Hindu religion. It means that the god in me recognizes the god in you. Or, I see you. Or the Divine in me recognizes the Divine in you.

Many Natives Americans tribes were very spiritual. I read that one of the first religious priests to observe the Sioux tribe, said "these people live the bible and they have never even seen it." I am assuming he meant the good parts of the bible that promote love. The Sioux tribe referred to their journey through life as walking the red road. This meant that they thought highly of being good people and tried to live their lives as good human beings. I have attended modern day sun dance. These folks often times fast. They do without food and often times water and dance in the sun. I believe in this way it is possible to connect with the sun in much the same way as I did while meditating on my picnic table when I experienced a million pin point light bulbs going off in my head. Sun dance allows the dancer to become one with the light. And, many tribes believe god is the sun and call god the great spirit or tonkashula.

Native Americans often put to practice the idea of oneness, and how it could be used to their advantage. For example, the whole village would collectively do sun dance by focusing their energy (thoughts) by praying for sun, they knew that they could in fact bring the sun out with this method. And they knew they could bring rain the same way with rain dance. And they also knew that we are all connected, in other words they knew we are all **One**. And they planned their life around that idea. In other words, knowing that we are all one gave them a profound respect for mother earth, nature and everything on mother earth. They demonstrated this belief in that everything was sacred to them. They believed that everything has a life has a spirit has a name. They referred to god as the great spirit. Many tribes did not even pick fruit from the vine without giving thanks and praise or giving loving thoughts to the source of energy that was to nourish them. In other words, extending gratitude towards their source of food.

I had an experience one time while living in New Mexico. It was not long after I had read a book which made, what seemed like on odd statement at the time. It seemed odd, because I was raised catholic, and it was counter to everything I was taught in catholic school. In the book It asks the reader to picture a **wheel with spokes**, it went on to say that god is the light, (the sun) and is at the center of the wheel. And it said that all god's children are somewhere on the spokes of this wheel. And in this manner, we are all connected. **We are all one.** Nikola Tesla said that **we are to the universe as a wave is to the ocean. We are all part of the whole.**

However, as a recovering catholic. I was having a hard time wrapping my head around this new age spiritual thought of oneness. So, I sat in my back yard on the picnic table in the sun to meditate. I was trying to wrap my mind around that idea. I was pondering this new idea of god. I was under the impression that god was a man in the sky somewhere watching us all the time. As I began to meditate and get in my zone, I suddenly experienced within my head, a **million pin point light bulbs** going off in my mind's eye. It seemed like it came directly from the light (sun). And, I believe at that point all my chakras were activated. I felt as though this was an affirmation of the idea that we are all part of the light and we are all one. Words simply can't describe what an experience that was.

I have to say that was a true enlightenment. No one can ever tell me god is not the light, and we are light and part of god. Maybe there is a man standing behind the sun, but I know that the light has something to do with it. I will always believe that god is pure love light and energy. And, we are part of the equation in that when we express love through our thoughts and behavior, because of the vibrations that we give off, we are expressing god. If we use our energy to express love than we are expressing god. For it is through us that god is expressed. That is to say we express god with vibrations of love. God is love light and energy. That profound experience was another **wink and a nod from the universe**, god or the great spirit. Call it what you want but we are all part of it.

Through all of my experiences, I began to relate many of the songs of the peace and love generation referred to as the counterculture. Or more commonly known as the hippies. I was reminded of a song that John Lennon wrote called **Imagine.**

Imagine all the people living life as <u>ONE.</u> Another song that came to mind was the song written by Joni Mitchell and popularized by Crosby Stills Nash and Young. The song is called the **Woodstock song.** These words ring a bell with me. **We are stardust we are golden we are ten-billion-year-old carbon, and we have got to get ourselves back to the garden. Carl Sagan** said we are star stuff. We are made up of the same stuff as the sun which is considered a star. We are made up of atoms of carbon, nitrogen, and hydrogen. Almost every element on earth was formed at the heart of a star.

CHAPTER 19

PROOF ENOUGH FOR US

I have been so fortunate to be a big part of my daughter's life, as I lived with her and her boys for a very long time, this gave me the opportunity to spend lots of time with my three grandsons. And by now, since my son had crossed over, I knew the importance of giving the boys love by way of giving them my time. And, fortunately, thanks to my daughter, I didn't have to work so much. So, I had plenty of time to dedicate to them. The boys and I grew very close because I was the designated babysitter. I helped my daughter raise them. The boys were forced to walk with me when they were little guys. I was an avid walker for many years and they had to tag along, I couldn't leave them alone as I was the babysitter. As they grew older and we had occasion to walk together, it was not uncommon for us to use our collective energy to bring out the sun when it was cloudy. I can't recall a time when it did not work, even if the sun peeked out if only for a moment. My middle grandson became my walking partner into his teenage years and now he is a runner and still practices this idea of bringing out the sun.

I believe Native Americans understood quantum physics without naming it. Quantum physics makes a strong case for the idea that our thoughts create our reality. And I believe that our collective thoughts create our collective reality. They knew that if they needed sun for example, the whole village would participate in the sun dance by focusing their energy (thoughts) by praying for sun, they knew that they could in fact bring the sun out with this method. And they also knew that we are all connected in other words they knew we are all One. And they planned their life around that idea. In other words, knowing that we are all one gave them a profound respect for mother earth, nature, and everything on earth. They believed that everything has a life has a spirit has a name. They demonstrated this belief, in that everything was sacred to them. They referred to god as the great spirit. Many tribes did not even pick food from the vine without giving thanks and praise to the fruit tree that supplied them with nourishment.

CHAPTER 20

THE LAW OF CONSERVATION OF MASS

Einstein said that "everything is energy", and **that's all there is**. Everything in the universe is made up of energy. The law of conservation of mass is basically saying that the mass (weight) of the universe is the same now as it always has been. Energy cannot be created or destroyed just change form. We are energy because that's all there is, according to Einstein. So basically, we have always been here in some form, since we are energy. We share the same energy that's always existed. Since we share the same energy it makes sense to keep our thought waves of a high frequency and spread love and compassion. When we make someone feel good, we are adding positive energy to the collective and benefiting ourselves as well. In some form we have always been here we just keep on evolving spiritually and coming back to the earth plane, (by choice) until we vibrate so highly, that we don't have to come back. This law of conservation of mass makes a good case for reincarnation.

I think that the point at which we don't have to come back to earth and do it again is perhaps when someone is vibrating at a number 9, with regard to numerology. Number 9 has the highest vibrational frequency except for the master number 11. Rather than come back for more lessons, maybe we then become angels and help to guide people from that other realm. I have heard that some of the spiritually evolved folks can levitate. I have heard it's possible.

Perhaps Jesus vibrated so highly that he could walk on water. His halo could have been from being filled with so much light that it appeared as a halo. Jesus was defiantly an ascended master.

At this point I must share an experience I had. One night I was listening to my favorite late-night radio talk show that delves into the unusual. This particular night they were discussing John Lennon and how he was into numerology and that his number was **number 9**. They were discussing all of the synchronicities in John Lennon's life with regard to the number 9. The next morning, I went next door to ask my brother, if he was aware that John Lennon was into numerology and that his number was **9**. Anyway, my brother being the rock trivia buff that he was answered immediately " Yes." He made the song **number 9, number 9, number 9**.

Aww, yes that's right I thought. I then made my way back to my trailer next door. As I approached the front door, I heard my phone ring and I ran back to my room to answer it and as I picked it up, I saw that it had **all 9s** across the screen. It blew my mind. And there was no one on the line when I answered it. Now all this took place when my mind was engrossed in the current events of the day. The threat of war and the possibility of bringing back the draft was looming in my mind. It was after **9/11** and the powers that be were amping up support for attacking Iraq. Later referred to as shock and awe. My grandsons were a big part of my life and I simply couldn't imagine these 3 gentle souls being convinced that it's ok to kill people for some deep dark political objective. Or be killed for deep state agenda. In fact, they were attending peace rallies with me as we were allowed to protest the invasion of Iraq for 2 hours every Saturday in a neighboring suburb to where we lived. At most maybe 40 left over hippies and some other folks who were concerned and had the time to be active in protesting war.

On the drive to the area where we had permission to be active against the impending war, I would play my old hippy music so my grandkids would hear how the music back in the day was still relevant. I remember playing the song that was popularized during the Viet Nam war. The song was called "Eve of Destruction." The guy sang with such passion that he brought tears to my little grandson's eyes. **"Old enough to kill but not for voting, you don't believe in war but what's that gun your totin".**

I graduated in 1968. The war was raging on. I knew so many young men that were drafted to go to Viet Nam right after graduation. They should have been enjoying the summer and their new freedom from the discipline of school. Some never came home. And some are still a mess after that war. PTSD can devastate someone's life. I remember Mohammed Ali went to jail for refusing to go to that war. He basically said he didn't want to go kill these little people in the jungle that he didn't know and had nothing against. Many people said he was a coward. He was not afraid to fight in the ring though. Like many others he was a conscientious objector. It makes sense to me. I think he was rather brave.

I guess that is what we were doing by holding signs and protesting the inevitable drums of war that the warmongers were pounding. I held a sign that said "Honk for peace." It gave me great satisfaction to hear the people honk, when they would be stopped at the busy intersection that we were allowed to hold our signs at. It was at these times when the stop light was red and people were able to read the signs, that most people would just lay on their horns. If nothing else it let me feel the pulse the American people with regard to war. And it kept the awareness in people's minds that we are once again going to war. One thing the draft was good for was forcing everyone to be engaged in the politics of war in the late 60's and 70's.

The 9/11 incident had taken place and brought out a lot of fear in the American people. It also occurred to me that the twin towers look like 11s. And it happened on 9/11. And when we have a crisis, we call 9/11. There is usually fear associated with having to dial 9/11. It seems there are a lot of man-made synchronicities there. As I say this, I am reminded of another song from back in the day from **The Who**, It goes like this **"Just like yesterday I'll get on my knees and pray we won't be fooled again"**. It was a good song but sadly we have been, and continue to be fooled into war. It seems the powers that be always have a reason to go to war. Yet they never go. So many of the songs of yesterday pointed out opposition to war. Another song that Scott McKenzie sang, some of the words are, **"The rulers wage the wars and our children fight and die. How did it happen how were we played for fools, and win with our children's lives in a game that has no rules?"**

I don't think the American people would have allowed the invasion of Iraq and the bombing of that country were it not that 9/11 occurred, we were fearful of another attack, and we had to retaliate. All I know is that it is just another reason for war.

At the time we were protesting war, the American people were being led to believe that Iraq was tied to 9/11, and that we had to go bomb them because they had weapons of mass destruction and we had to spread democracy. And we did go bomb them to the extent that we refer to it as shock and awe. Yet, no weapons were ever found there. Some people believe it was an inside job. If a guy watches Fahrenheit 9/11, you can't help but wonder. Most American people are good at heart and would never allow the bombing of another country for no reason.

Americans were misled and fear is a tool to gain approval for war. I think we have been played for fools throughout history. We have been lied into wars. Human beings are so honorable they will jump to the call of duty when it comes to protecting their families. Often times they are misguided by not so well-intentioned beings, like the powers that be. A guy has to admit there have always been warmongers running the world. Constant wars.

At the time this looming threat of the invasion of Iraq was taking place, I was doing a lot of contemplating on the idea of war. And I was doing automatic writing. By that I mean I was writing poems that seemed to just be flowing from my heart to my hand. I was very engaged in the idea of protesting war and all the hidden agenda of the powers that be. My take is that either the spirit world (my son) or God, or the universe or good aliens with their technical skills were somehow listening or watching me and were perhaps giving their approval with regard to my dedication to express my thoughts regarding war. I don't have any other explanation for the number 9 appearing across the screen on my little cheapie phone.

I don't mind bringing up at this point, once again that many wars are able to take place because government creates scenarios which perpetuate collective thoughts of fear. I said before I don't think that Americans, would ever have allowed the bombing of Baghdad or Iraq had it not been preceded by 9/11. A perfect example of fear being used as a tool so that evil acts are not questioned. In **2003** our country bombed Iraq, with such a vengeance that it was named shock and wave. One excuse was that there was the threat of weapons of mass destruction somewhere there. In retrospect, I would have to conclude that the fear that was perpetuated from the powers that be and their use of media, allowed the bombing of Iraq to go on because we were kept in fear with regard to another attack like 9/11. Oh yes, and to spread democracy, that was another reason that we allowed the bombing of Iraq.

However, my thoughts with regard to the idea of spreading democracy is that it (democracy) must come bubbling from within. And, isn't it odd that 911 is also the number used for emergency calls? Both numbers 911 and 9/11 both bring up fearful thoughts.

I do think that the number 9 with regard to its spiritual meaning describes John Lennon. As I stated before the number 9 represents completion. Perhaps his earthly journey was complete. Much of his musical career was spent dedicating his music to the importance of expressing love on planet earth. He would draw huge crowds when giving a concert and expressing opposition to war, social injustice and the status quo. If he were alive today, he would still be passionate about helping humanity question war and the status quo. He would be instrumental in bringing about peace with his music. The fact that there was a draft that took place made war more of an issue. Nobody wanted to go to Vietnam. If your number came up you were drafted to go to the military. There were a lot of people that had skin in the game. Nobody wants to go to war. Brave men do it because of their sense of duty to protect their families and the American people in general. Like another song from back in the day. "**War, what is it good for, absolutely nothing.**" Perhaps that is why John Lennon was killed. I don't think he will have to come back to earth plane. He can guide us from the heavenly realm.

It seems that every time there is a person that draws a large crowd, and can unite the people like John Lennon did, they end up dead. People like Ghandi, Martin Luther King, Kennedy.

John Lennon's music resonated with so many people. His songs were powerful. He was a peace activist because of his music. It is sad we lost over 55,000 young men in that war. Not to mention the casualties on the other side. There were so many artists back in the day, that questioned war and the status quo.

Pink Floyd sang a song called **Us, Us, Us, and Them, Them, Them**. The video that is associated with the song depicts us as the people, marching like good workers to the mines and solders marching off the war. On the other hand, it shows them, the rulers who wage the wars playing golf while the good people are Marching to the tune of the drums of war like good sheeple. Something is wrong with that picture. It has happened throughout history. It seems that throughout history the elite have taken advantage of the average hard-working person. This to the point that children were once exploited and child labor laws had to be implemented. Some children are exploited in other countries today by the powerful. All for money.

CHAPTER 21

CONSCIOUSNESS

Consciousness is the ability to be aware of oneself and one's surroundings. In other words, it is the ability to take in information. The way we do this is through the 5 senses. We take in information through the 5 senses the brain then decodes this information into our reality. For example, the reason we hear music or language is that this information comes in the form of vibrational sound waves. The waves hit the ear drum and the parts in the inner ear hammer out the vibrations against the drum, according to their frequency.

You can't see the sound waves because they are invisible vibrations, but your brain decodes the information based on their frequency. The same thing with smell you can't see smells but the nose takes in the information and the brain decodes it. So, consciousness is information. We can't see the information because they are waves or frequencies but they are there. There are all kinds of waves we are bombarded with but we don't see. For example, the WYFI, we can't see these waves until they are received and decoded and ultimately made visible on the screen. Radio waves exist but we can't see them. We can't even hear them until our radio station is tuned in to the frequency of our choice. There is so much that exists but is unseen. In fact, we are only able to see what exists in our range of frequency. So much information is available that is unseen. We only have a small range of visible light with which to view our reality. Remember, that's why the spirit world cannot be seen very often. They occupy the same space but they are vibrating on a different frequency than we are.

Nikola Tesla said everything is energy, frequency, and vibration. Everything is made up of atoms and everything is vibrating. Including us. Even though we can't see the vibrations of matter, all matter is vibrating, even mother earth.

Everything is made up of atoms. Scientists that look at atoms have discovered that atoms are mostly empty space. The question that this information presented was how can we be made up atoms, when atoms are mostly empty space. Physicists have come to the conclusion that matter is not solid. What we see as physical is actually vibrating information at different frequencies in the form energy, that our brains decode as our reality. All that exists is information, in the form of electromagnetic waves. All information is wave form. We are consciousness in different states of perception. Einstein said reality is an illusion all be it a persistent one.

Scientists have concluded by studying the things that make up atoms, called sub atomic particles, (protons, electrons and neutrons) that it is only when there is an observer does the energy wave collapse and becomes a particle with infinite possibilities. However, the possibilities are limited to what our 5-sense reality can pick up. We are limited to our 5 sense possibilities. Hence, the saying "if a tree falls in the forest and no one is there to hear it, does it make a sound?" As the tree falls, it whizzes through the air as it falls causing disturbance in the energy field, but if no one is there to decode it then it did not make a sound. It is as though we are consciousness playing avatars having a virtual reality. In other words, reality is consciousness at different states of perception. The way we interact with the universe is waveform. Our perception is the creator of our reality. Information comes as wave form and how we decode it has to do with our perception. I believe that our perception has been hijacked by the powers that be. They have fed us information through the news, religion and the education system, that has influenced our perception of reality.

CHAPTER 22

ONTOLOGICAL MATHEMATICS

O ntological mathematics is the science that proves the truth that the world is not material but a collective dream, that "matter" is an illusion, and the ultimate reality is a domain of pure mind. This is a mathematical certainty. Ontological mathematics is the study of the mathematical wave nature of existence. This reality is not a reality of matter, rather it's a reality of mind, of thought.

Thoughts are mathematical sinusoidal waves. Ontological mathematics studies the mathematical waveforms of mind that make up all of existence and you're very being. This spacetime world which we live in isn't a material reality at all.

It's the Holos. The Holos is a mathematical Fourier projection from a frequency singularity known as the Source. You are a mind. Existence is a thought. The world is a Dream. A collective dream or a grand thought. If you think about it when we are dreaming, we see people materialize in our dreams as if they exist. In this same way we believe we exist. This reality we are sharing is like a dream. A grand dream. And when we dream, we are having a dream within a dream. We are actually a collection of sinusoidal waves, thoughts. A mind, a soul is a collection of sinusoidal waves. Sinusoidal waves are not just carrying energy and information but they are mind and life itself. Sinusoidal waves are the essence of reality. For mind to exist mind must be present in the fundamental constituents of existence. Mind did not spring from matter, matter springs from mind. Empirical scientists say that knowledge is gained through observation and the senses. They cannot see the mind, therefore they can't measure it so they believe that matter came first then the mind.

My understanding of this process as explained by a brilliant young man who calls himself Morgue. He has a brilliant way of explaining this whole process so that someone with very limited understanding can wrap their head around.

He explains that the source is the sun, god or the universal mind. My experience by using the pendulum and the dowsing rods leads me to believe that the universal mind is what we can tap in to, when using these tools.

The sun pours out the thoughts of the cosmic mind into spacetime reality. We are part of the source part of the sun, the light. We are light. And matter is transformed light. Photons are thought particles. Light and mind have the same properties, in that they are both massless.

A mind a soul is a collection of sinusoidal waves or frequencies or thoughts, and are the essence of existence. Mental activity is the prerequisite for life. Just like when your dreaming you need thought and thinking for the dream world to happen. The dream world is an image or a representation of thought and thinking. So, this reality is a representation of thought and thinking. Collective thoughts and thinking. All of our thought and thinking interacting together. This is what forms an interference pattern. The interference pattern is what gives rise to structure. Since we are light, this is where Fourier transforms occurs which give rise to the hologram. Interference pattern gives rise to a structured hologram. Our thoughts when they interact together as minds as souls, because we are light that is what gives rise to the interference pattern which constructs reality.

At the fundamental level of quantum mechanics, you get interference patterns. When you look at so called matter at the quantum mechanical level you see interference pattern, which are the property of waves. At the fundamental quantum level matter starts behaving like waves, and we get interference patterns. We as minds as souls, because we are light are minds as sinusoids and our interaction together is what gives rise to the collective interference patterns of existence. Existence is a grand thought or grand wave function. The universal wave function. Thoughts are photons, and suns pour out the thoughts of the cosmic mind in to space time and matter, and black holes restore space time thoughts to their origin in the source the singularity origin.

All of this information is available including the formula. Morgue has books explaining all this in full detail. I gravitate to this information as it supports my belief that the sun is the source (god) and we are all part of it. Math and logic are the basis for explaining the process. Morgue also introduces the idea of hyperianism. **Ontological mathematics is the rational core of hyperianism.** The mathematical system that will replace science and religion. The current system of capitalism and consumerism have influenced humanity in negative ways. Hyperianism seeks to create a new system of reason, logic, and compassion. A system where everyone is given a chance to self-actualize. And that's what I am talking about.

CHAPTER 23

ILLUSION

I have often heard that life is but an illusion. I already understood that our thoughts create our reality. The visual experiment that showed how good thoughts on water droplets created beautiful snowflake like designs, and how focusing negative thoughts had the opposite effect on the water I began to see how our collective thoughts have created our current collective experience since we are all connected. Like Nikola Tesla said, we are to the universe as a wave is to the ocean. We are all part of the whole. We are all important we are all a part of the puzzle and we all have a part to play in this grand design.

I began to see more clearly how our collective reality must be a result of improper thinking since we are having a dystopian like experience on this planet. The idea is that if we only had positive thoughts coming from love we would create a paradise.

I began to relate the two pillars resembling two 11's in the temple of the descending gods, were the reflections of the collective thoughts of each society. Each pillar reflecting opposite realities, thus opposite thought patterns. Each pillar resembling a pathway, and indicating a choice or free will.

Love is what we are born with, fear is what we learn. We are introduced to fear from the first day we were born. Think of how we use to be introduced to the world at birth. The first thing the doctor would do is give you a whack on you bottom. Ouch. Imagine that. That's no way to be introduced into the world. Worse than that imagine yourself a boy child being born in the western world, and being circumcised shortly after birth. Not a good way to be introduced into the world. I saw no reason to allow them to do that to my son. I saw no reason to distrust the intelligent design of the universe.

Once again, I was meditating on the idea of illusion and this new age way of thinking. I was trying to wrap my mind around this idea. As I was meditating on the idea of illusion, it was then that my son gave me a sigh that he was still with me, guiding me along. The song "Carry on my wayward son" by Kansas, popped into my head. The lyrics that I heard in my head were as follows.

> Carry on my wayward son
> They'll will be peace when you are done
> Lay your weary head to rest
> Don't you cry no more no
> Once I rose above the noise
> And confusion just to get a glimpse
> Beyond this **illusion**
> I was soaring ever higher
> But I flew to high

The synchronicity of the song and how it related to my son and his crossing over made it clear in my mind that this reality is and illusion and that my son and the universe were giving me a wink and a nod that I must pay attention to. My son was soaring ever higher as he had more pain killers in his system than had been prescribed by the doctors for his upper respiratory condition as he had strep throat at the time of his death. But he flew too high.

His body died but his soul his spirit (energy) lives on and his spirit will never die. Energy never dies it just changes form.

I know this song was put in my consciousness by my son. The experience confirmed for me that this life experience is an illusion brought about by improper thinking and all that really exists is love.

That is because when ego and all its negative connotations are removed all there is left is love. I believe that when we die our spirit raises up and only the high vibrations of love are lifted with the spirit, and the negative stays here on earth. Maybe that's why poltergeists and angry ghosts haunt various places, especially when some sort of atrocity was committed in the area where the apparition occurs. I say this remembering to be on this dimension we are the ground for positive and negative energy, yin and yang. And energy never dies just changes form.

Our planet seems to be experiencing a lot of fear at this point in time in history, Covid-19 most recently. The unusual weather that is occurring all over the planet could be a reflection of the turmoil that people are faced with. It seems to me that some of the worst weather often visits the bible belt. Perhaps that is because there are so many people who are god **fearing**. Perhaps all that concentrated fear affects the weather. Fear includes the negative emotion called judgement. Love is the absence of judgement. Religion involves judgement by god and us as well. The powers that be keep us in a constant state of fear. Meditation is important to reach our higher selves (the god in each of us), and ask that our thought forms be purified. We must be clear about our intention when meditating. If our intentions are to add love to the collective, then we will probably be going through the dark night of the soul. In order to elevate the vibrations of the collective we must work on ourselves. My meditations are sometimes very helpful as I am confronted with the things that I have done wrong that has ended up hurting someone. It's as though my subconscious has recorded all my negative behavior and runs it past me during some of my meditations. It reminds me of the people who have near death experiences and say that their whole life flashes before them. I have heard this process of record keeping is referred to as The Akashic Records. In any case as I am remembering the deeds of life, I say the prayer "I'm sorry please forgive me thank you and I love you." I put out that healing energy of forgiveness and love to the universe and it adds to the collective and raises the vibrations of the collective. It's a healing energy as I forgive myself for being human, because I know that we as humans are the ground for the positive and negative energy that must exist for us to manifest on this planet. The idea is to live in Christ Consciousness and clean up our souls and thoughts and remember that we are all one. By doing this we will elevate the vibrations of the world and ascend together to another dimension. This will happen when we reach a critical mass of those living in Christ Consciousness.

Now is the time we are in the age of Aquarius so it is we who must do the work and let love steer the stars like the song Aquarius suggests.

CHAPTER 24

CAPITALISM

This is what I do know. The bible says the root of all evil is the love of money. The money lovers are running the world. It seems where ever you have money you have the money lovers. This rings true because money provides the atmosphere where by greed can be expressed. And, is being expressed every day all over the world. The earth the air the water and the food have all been compromised for the root of all evil (money). We have war for profit too.

Many stockholders have no idea how their money is being invested. For example, many stockholders aren't aware that their money is being invested in various chemical products that are destructive to the environment, our food and our health. So, it seems that the quest for money trumps the importance of our health. The bible says that "it's hard for the rich to get to heaven." I can see why, because money is more important than mankind. Money becomes the god of the money lovers. They even put it in your face. It's on our dollar bill. In god we trust. I sometimes wonder how some super rich people can sleep at night, knowing that there are people starving. I have witnessed what I consider to be vulgar displays of wealth, when compared to the suffering of some unfortunate folks. The root of all evil is the love of money. It seems as though the money lovers are running the show for all of us.

The government officials who are elected by the people are actually carrying out the agenda for the beings that benefit by keeping us in fear. The hidden hand that runs the world. The hand that loves war. The hand that has designed a world full of chaos and separation. They pull the strings for both right wing and left-wing government officials. Right wing and left wing come from the same bird. and they have little regard for the earth or the people inhabiting the earth. One side pretends to care about the commonwealth in the name of democracy. They might throw the poor a bone now and then to throw us off into thinking that they care. But nothing really changes. The other side claims to be fiscally responsible, but they don't mind spending trillions on war. The best way to be fiscally responsible is to put an end to war.

Nothing really changes no matter who is in place as leaders. There is still war and still hunger and still homelessness and suffering all over this planet. These things exist no matter who our elected officials are at any given point in time. That is why it's easy to imagine a hidden hand that runs the entire world. It is called the illuminati. Or deep state. I think capitalism would actually work for us as a country, or for the rest of the world that uses this system, if the money lovers weren't running the world.

These same money lovers are the same ones that want to spread capitalism in favor of communism. And they don't mind sending you to war for it. I remember as a child being afraid of the communists. We had drills at school where we had to get under the table in case we were to be bombed. People were building bomb shelters because we were engaging verbally in a war like manner with Russia. We were taught that capitalism is the way the world should conduct their business. And this idea was worth going to war for and bombing the hell out of innocent people who have no choice in the matter. The fear factor was alive and well ever since I can remember. Yet I can't remember ever knowing a Russian or hating one. Yet, we were conditioned to fear them enough to go to war with them.

It doesn't seem that communism works very well either though. Perhaps communism would work if it wasn't for the idea that there is a hidden hand running that way of government as well. It seems the leaders of that type of government live very well and have the best of everything. I think the leaders of the industrial world always live like royalty. I read that the streets had to be cleared of all the homeless and needy where the royal wedding procession took place. It seems they are pretending that these problems don't exist if they hide them. I guess it would seem obvious by comparison, just how ridiculous this scenario is. It would simply be too much in the face of the observers of the royal procession, if the needy people were visible. That's kind of a vulgar display of wealth when compared to the poverty that exists.

I think we treat the members of our government that are calling the shots for all of us like royalty. They have the best health care they make a lot of money compared to us, and they usually get rich while they are in office. Often times they are rich going in to office. And they make the laws that send us to wars and to jail if we break the laws. Yet they often times seem to be above the law. Now, how are rich people going to understand what it is like to struggle. I think we need ordinary men in office because they understand the struggles of ordinary life. Our leaders lead anything but ordinary lives. And they are tempted by pay offs by the hidden hand.

The only people that get in office are the people who are going to continue with the status quo. That would be continuous war, keeping people in fear by way of poverty, and reducing the quality of people's lives in general. If people are struggling to make a living, there is little time or energy to question the status quo.

The problems I just mentioned could be solved if the leaders had intention of doing so. We could in fact be able to accomplish what the words to this song says. I'm referring to the song by Stevie Miller Band **"Shoe the children with no shoes on their feet, house the people living in the street, oh oh there's a solution."** Many of the solutions are obvious and simple. One of the many issues that could be tackled by society to help alleviate hunger in the inner cities is to grow food in the inner cities instead of foliage that provides only beauty. I see so many empty buildings that could house the people that don't want to live in the streets. Homeless people could also help with renovation projects for housing purposes. They could restore abandoned buildings. Perhaps in return for food and shelter the folks that would otherwise be hungry, and homeless, could tend to the care and harvesting of the crops that would grow in the cities.

Other issues could be tackled by better preparing our youth for real life situations. I am totally convinced that schools should focus on teaching children how to grow gardens. We are so removed from having control of what we put in our mouths. We are conditioned to let unscrupulous people grow our food. Those that put money before the welfare of mankind. A great deal of our food is being grown and genetically modified by the largest pesticide manufacture in the world. It is referred to as roundup ready. Round up is a dangerous chemical.

In junior high school I was taught how to make a skirt in sewing class, which was part of home economics. In high school we made a dress. I don't see any of this nowadays. My brothers made a table in wood shop. Youngsters should be taught how to change their car oil. Also, they should teach kids how to change the tires on their car. Practical skills should be taught once again.

I believe that the elite the billionaires many times over those beings who could throw a billion dollars in the toilet and never miss it, actually design the laws that create chaos and fear and keep us divided. They create loopholes and ways of getting out of paying taxes themselves. This puts a heavier burden on the upper middleclass, many whom have gone to school and worked hard all their lives. They now have a comfortable life, and resent being taxed higher than others just because they make more money. You can't blame them either, their happiness is tied to having a level of comfort that allows them to enjoy more travel, more toys etc. They deserve to enjoy the quality of life they have worked hard for. They have played by the rules of capitalism. They function well in capitalism.

So, the burden of taking care of the needy should not be disproportionately left up to them. The superrich (1%) (the hidden hand) should pick up the slack there, instead of designing laws to get out of contributing to the welfare of the masses. Especially since it would not be a burden to them or lower their level of comfort in any way.

Often times I have heard the hardworking people who make decent money complain and say "why should I have to take care of people who don't work". Their thinking is I have worked hard all my life to get where I am. They don't think that they should be burdened with a societal issue that they didn't create. They played by the rules of the game. They are right too. They are the ones who function well in capitalism, and they may say "I'm fine in this system, I do well with capitalism". And they do. They have adjusted well. Or have they? I have come to the conclusion that **It is no measure of health to be well adjusted to a sick society**. I think a person could take that literally, as I do, because there are so many folks that have some kind of illness that dictates, they take medications of some kind.

Perhaps we would all be healthier if we remembered we are all part of the same energy that **Is, was and always will be**. Everything is energy and that's all there is. Even thoughts have energy. We are all part of the infinite mind. The universal consciousness. We are all One. If one person is suffering then we all suffer in some way as we share the same energy. I say this because we are all part of the same energy that exists and has always existed. If we share this energy it is in our best interest to influence the collective energy in a positive loving way. We are to the universe as a wave is to the ocean. Part of the Whole, thus we are ONE.

It is becoming harder and harder to survive with a level of comfort now days unless you have been established for years. Especially in the cities. It is no wonder that the candidate who proposed socialized medicine and free education drew so many young people willing to vote for him. If you think about it we already have many social programs. For example, the fire and police departments, and public-school systems for starters. We need to extend this to health care and education. This would alleviate a lot of stress many people experience, and add to the negative energy that we all share. This reminds me of another song from way back when. These random words to the 1967 song titled: Let's Live For Today, by the Grass Roots apply to today's society more than ever. (**"When I think of all the worries people seem to find and how they're in a hurry to complicate their mind, by chasing after money and dreams that can't come true." "We were never meant to worry the way the that people do."**)

If you can afford to buy a house now days or rent one it takes at least 2 pay checks to pay the mortgage or the rent. And, if you have student loans you could be struggling most of your life. And, of course moms have to work now too. This condition seriously reduces the quality of life for the masses. And it makes for a lot of latch key kids. We are conditioned to accept a lifestyle that compromises the welfare of our children. It's time to wake up. Often times we live in fear of not being able to make ends meet.

Most folks are conditioned to know that they are probably going to have to get a job and work the rest of their lives to make a living and survive with a roof over their heads and food in their stomachs. Most folks don't question this existence they are just happy to have a job or two, and look forward to the weekend. Most folks are just content to make ends meet. People are conditioned to think that this is the way it is. However, it is becoming increasingly harder to make ends meet for the average person. The struggle reduces the quality of life for everyone since we are all one and sharing the energy that exists. I loved this song it gained popularity in the 80's. It was called We Are The World. Most people will remember the words, **"We are the world we are the children. There's a choice we're making were saving our own lives, its true we make a brighter day so let's start giving."** The words to the song indicate the author of the lyrics clearly understood we are all one by helping others we are saving ourselves.

I try to carry a couple dollars in the ash tray of my car. I do this because there are so many people on street corners begging for money. Some people have criticized me for doing so. They argue that the people begging can get a job and they are lazy and they are probably just going to get a bottle of booze. It's all in how you look at it. I look at it as though this **is** his job to be there in the street begging for money. By that I mean maybe it's his karma to remind us of how sick society has become. Perhaps his purpose is to put it in our face and see if it wakes us up to the idea that our current capitalistic system is failing. I don't want to spend time or energy trying to determine if this unfortunate person begging for money deserves it. If I contribute to his getting a bottle then I can live with that. I put the energy of love out there. And, maybe the guy is hungry. He can get a burger with a couple of dollars. It's a personal decision and my way of helping. And it's something I can afford.

I actually learned this behavior from my son before he died. I once saw him take a handful of change from his pocket as we were stopped at a light. He dropped it down on the ground to help a guy begging for cash. The light had changed and we couldn't wait for the guy to approach, so my son just dropped the change on the ground for the guy. I remember telling my son that the guy probably won't be able to recover the money. However, he looked back and said "he gave us a thumbs up mom," and he is picking up the coins. He is smiling mom. I know that my son probably learned the positive ripple effects of a compassionate act like that when he was in the streets. There were those times I tried to enforce tough love on my son when he was drugging and I am sure he was the benefactor of someone's kind act, when he ended up in the street himself. I believe in doing small acts of kindness with great love.

The definition of love in the metaphysical world is the absence of judgement. It takes energy to judge. Energy should be spent on important issues, rather than judgment. Perhaps these unfortunate homeless people lack the confidence or self-esteem or other tools that it takes to accomplish the task of getting a job. Or maybe they are there to remind us that this society is sick and we should have different priorities. We need to put out the loving vibrations and not judge them. However, we need to focus on providing them with the tools that help them to help themselves. Judgement is not loving these folks. Love thy neighbor as thyself. If we don't have the ability or mindset to help them, then give them a silent blessing, and move on. That's ok too. In order to love one's self, one must not judge oneself. No one is perfect. We must have compassion for ourselves and then we can apply this virtue to others. We all make mistakes, and we all have different paths, but in the end, we are all one.

We are all part of that infinite consciousness, the realm where we are all One and only love exists. The realm where we all go when we die. the realm where there is only love, all ego has been removed. The realm where we see what effect our ego driven lives have had on the world. We then decide out of love to come back and learn. We are all part of that one pool of consciousness that we can tap into through various ways including meditation, divining rods or the pendulum. In any case we are all part of it. It is better to have a positive ripple effect on the world than to add a negative ripple effect.

I think that modern society that is based on capitalism is producing so much chaos and fear that its effecting every aspect of our lives. Our current experience on the planet is chaotic in so many aspects. There is so much war and poverty and racism and hate and fear on the planet. The energy of fear on a collective level, is the same energy that is causing so much bad weather. There are wild fires, (reflecting anger) and floods, (reflecting the tears of mother earth) tornados, (reflecting chaos). If the super-rich would just open their pocket books and work to alleviate the suffering of the human race, and step up to the plate and share, they could save the human race. They could afford to take a hit for the team. They wouldn't even feel the hit. Apparently, it's not an option for them. They are not on the same team.

Capitalism actually puts women against men in as much as it provides the environment whereby women compete in the workplace place with men. After WWII, women were no longer satisfied with being housewives. Convenience, and technology began to shape the world in a different way. Technological conveniences left more time on women's hands. She could now do her chores in half the time. All the while numerous consumer items were becoming available. So, women began to go to work to acquire that second car, or that Kirby vacuum, or that new sofa, or that automatic washer. I remember my auntie doing laundry with the wringer washer. You had to put each item through rollers to get as much water out so they could dry on the line. It became the era of keeping up with the Joneses. Now we are conditioned to the idea that working mothers is normal, when it didn't use to be that way. Turn key kids is normal now, I'm referring to children who return to an empty home after school. How can we raise children properly when we cannot focus on them? There is little time for nurturing and instilling values in children when both parents have to work. This is part of the diabolical plan to keep us pre-occupied and dumbed down.

Our economic society is set up to encourage companies to continually come out with useless consumer items that ultimately end up in the landfills... (plastic toys are one example). It seems to me we are destroying mother earth in so many ways. and **we have to get back to the garden**. These words remind me of the **Woodstock** song. The lines still apply to our world as I write this. This song is another example of how the peace and love generation nailed it with their music.

Random lines from the
Woodstock song

I came upon a child of god
he was walking along the road
and I asked him tell me where are you
goin this he told me
Well Im going down to Yasgur's farm
Gonna join in a rock and roll band
Got to get back to the land
To set my soul free
we are stardust we are golden
we are ten-billion-year-old carbon
AND WE'VE GOT TO GET OUSELVES
BACK TO THE GARDEN
I dreamed I saw the bomber jet planes
riding shot gun in the sky
turn into butterfly's above our nation

I often wonder how the top 1% percent of the population that hold most of the wealth can sleep at night, knowing there are so many folks doing without the basic things that allow for some quality of life. How can they knowingly disregard mother earth? It's as if they have no human feelings at all. Perhaps they **are not** human at all. I am referring the super-rich **(top 1%), those who** could literally throw millions in the toilet without missing it. If they had human qualities like compassion, and love of their fellow man they could not enjoy their level of comfort without feeling as though they should contribute to the welfare of mankind. I do not believe there are very many **humans** that would not display compassion for their fellow man, if they knew he was hungry or cold or visibly suffering if it was in their realm of possibilities to help. However, it may not be possible given the amount of fear that is inflicted upon us by the powers that be. Fear of not having enough can influence a person's decision to make the choice of helping someone or not helping.

We have been conditioned to accept man's inhumanity to man as the normal way of life. There are sick humans that inflict pain on others, but I can guarantee that they were abused themselves. However, the average person that was raised with any love at all are sensitive to the suffering of others. Most people are compassionate by nature if they were raised with love, but we are influenced by the fear that permeates the energy we share.

The powers that be keep us in fear and so busy trying to make a living, and in many cases struggling to do so. If we are busy then we have no time to wonder why things are the way they are. We have been conditioned to be good sheeple, we just go along like sheeple and question nothing. We are just happy to have a couple days off every week, to be with family, to relax and re-cooperate from the hassles of the work week. That would include for many, the drive to and from work, (traffic).

And the stress of making ends meet. People just want to relax on their days off and rest and have enough left over on their checks to do something enjoyable even if it's just to buy a six pack, or a little herb to help them relax and unwind. They are happy to have some rest till Monday comes along and start all over again. Sadly, there are many folks that never even get a day off, working two jobs does not allow it.

CHAPTER 25

CORPORATIONS

I know there are corporations worth billions of dollars and they pay slave labor wages. I know many people who make eleven dollars an hour, and they are working for corporations that literally make billions of dollars a year. Eleven dollars is the equivalent of slave wages in today's world. Especially here in Colorado. So many people have flocked here since recreational pot is now legal in the state of Colorado. The result is that real estate has gone up because of the demand. And, our freeways are flooded now. Many of these people remain homeless and still sleep in their cars, after working a forty-hour week. It's a shame that a guy working 40 hours a week, can't afford to rent a place to live. That is an example of how the large corporations that literally make billions of dollars a year in profits, have enslaved the working class.

I was blessed in my later years with my own business, whereby I didn't have to compete with corporations. It is hard to compete with corporations that pay slave labor wages. The last corporation I worked for I made eight dollars and fifty cents an hour plus tips. This took place in the early 90s. The owners were business people that could not cut hair. Yet they drove two very expensive cars with good tires. I clearly remember them calling me on a horrible snow day. They were complaining that I needed to come in and pull my shift. Well my response was that my tires were bald and they simply would not move my car. They were angry about that one. The truth is I could not afford the new tires. I think this is an example of how capitalism has a negative effect on mankind.

The corporate owners justified low wages with the idea that tips should increase our wages. However, that puts a burden on the average family that just want a haircut for themselves and their kids. And it's crazy that some huge well-known corporations pay their employees so low that they actually have to get food stamps to support themselves or their families. That is called corporate welfare. Many get out of paying taxes like we have to. I do not mind paying taxes if my tax money helps my brothers and sisters in the world. But I think corporations with huge profits should be paying their share of taxes rather than being instrumental in designing tax laws that render them free of any tax burden. They are better capable of adhering to the idea that we are our brother's keepers. They should feel obligated to pay a living wage.

Had I been able to drive to work as they demanded I would have endangered myself and everyone I encountered on the road. Corporate owners and stock holders simply must not realize that by denying the working class a living wage they actually endanger other people. I know that there are a lot of good people who just don't know how destructive capitalism is to the world. I am sure there are good responsible owners of corporations out there too, but not in the hair cutting business. They adhere to policy, and policies do not have a heart, only a bottom line.

A lot of good people just don't know how destructive capitalism is to the world. I think that there are entirely too many consumer items that tempt us and our children. I drive by people's houses on trash days, and there are so many plastic toys that end up in the trash and ultimately in the landfills. I think of all the cell phones and the computer games, and how they distract from more natural ways of entertainment. And so many disposable items that are harmful because of the very low vibrations like cell phones. It seems we live in a disposable world.

Many folks are doing without the very things that grant some quality of life to people. I'm referring to the folks that do not do well in a capitalistic society. Everyone deserves to have a nest. A place to sleep, food to eat, these things are so basic and grant some quality of life. I don't think we should be judging the folks that are unable to acquire these things for themselves. Some folks simply don't do well in this capitalistic society that produces so many issues and causes separation. We are **one** and we need to wake up to that idea so we can heal the planet. For the most part people want to work and be functional and do their best to succeed. Society has created the environment whereby healthy family settings are hard to come by since both parents are forced to work.

Most of my working life I spent working for corporations. Not so much by choice, but because corporations have put most small hair cutting places out of business. Later on in my life, I was lucky enough to have my own business within a truck stop. The truck stop provided a scenario whereby I didn't have to compete with a corporation. Once I was fortunate enough to have my own business, and not forced to comply with policy of corporations, I was able to express myself freely. Religion and politics are the issues I was told to never discuss while preforming my job while working for a corporation. This was corporate policy. You are never supposed to discuss these things. In other words, we were not allowed to discuss anything of true importance. Having my own business gave me the freedom to set my very affordable price of $10 dollars for a haircut. I could also set my own hours. This gave me the opportunity to make family issues more important than making money. Having my own business supplied me with the perfect podium for expressing my very strong views on religion, politics, and anything that fell under the umbrella of the unusual or paranormal. Having my own little business gave me the freedom to talk freely, and listen intensely. I say this because I have met some of the most intelligent folks who happen to be long haul truck drivers. I know that many of them listen to late-night talk radio stations to help them stay awake. Many truck drivers prefer driving at night. There is one particular night-time talk radio station that delves into such things as the paranormal, UFOs, conspiracy theories, spirituality, etc... I love discussing all of the above subjects, so I often find myself in the most interesting conversations with the drivers, since many of them are night drivers and listen to late night talk shows, where these subjects are on the air waves. Lots of out of the box subjects that are not normally discussed in the day time.

When I worked for corporations, they mostly wanted us to talk about products that they wanted us to push to enhance their profits. Increasing their profits did not concern me. I was more concerned with the fact that I was getting low wages and this was in the 90's. And yes, I worked hard so that I could increase my base pay. I got so good and fast I could cut 30 haircuts in an 8-hour shift. I am a hard worker and I'm proud of that but, I can't tell you what it does to the neck and back. But, as long as corporate was happy, I was expected to be satisfied. But of course, they weren't, because I did not push product. In fact, I would secretly tell the client that if they were concerned with the earth where they could get more earth friendly products. Or if they were not made out of money, I directed them to places where they could acquire less expensive products that do the same thing as the products that corporate would have me push.

CHAPTER 26

NO RELIGION TOO

Everyone probably remembers the song **"Imagine"** by John Lennon. All the words to the song resonate with me. However, I want to discuss a possible implication of certain words in the song. "Imagine there's no countries it isn't hard to do, nothing to kill or die for, **no religion too**". Imagine all the people living life in peace. Another song from back in the hippy days.

Many religious people truly believe that they will be blessed by interfering in the Middle East by supporting Israel. The man that ran for president, and was referred to as an old hippy said, "We will never have peace if we don't understand the Palestine issue." Many religious people truly believe that we are obligated to support Israel. They are just going by what the Bible has said and religious leaders support.

And the fact that no religious leaders ever make a stand against war and violence and ignore the fact that we are always warring somewhere makes me mistrust most conventional religious doctrines. Not that some of them don't mean well, but their priorities seem to be somewhere else. I submit to you that the mere fact that there **is** so many religions, is a form of separation in and of itself. There should be only one religion. The religion of Love and Oneness. There was a song entitled **"ONE LOVE"** by Bob Marley. He is dead now. Some people believe he was killed. It seems that all the great leaders that promote peace in my lifetime have been killed. **I believe they were** killed because they raised mass consciousness to the point that they became a threat to the status quo.

Many religions use fear to gain obedience. Fear of burning in hell, that is a pretty scary thought. If you have ever had a burn, then you know you want to avoid it, especially If it's going to last for eternity. What could be worse than burning in hell forever. Jesus said, **" do not fear"** and **"do not be afraid"** Yet it seems ironic that some religions use fearful thoughts as a tool to gain obedience. And, since fear is the opposite of love, and since a thought has energy and our collective thoughts have even more energy, that statement cannot be ignored. I say this because we are all connected and sharing energy. Energy cannot be created or destroyed, just change form. It is in our best interest to take care of one another when we can and to put out thoughts of love whenever we can.

I think that if we are (U.S.) going to police the world and involve ourselves in global politics than we must approach these issues from the standpoint of bringing about peace. War should simply not be an option. How can we as a so called "Christian Nation " even entertain the idea of war like solutions. This isn't a right wing or left-wing political issue, the right wing and the left wing come from the same bird. On second thought maybe war **is** indicative of a Christian nation. There is a common thread between countries that war and certain conventional religions. This has been true throughout history. I wonder how many people have died or been tortured in the name of god. War is barbaric, it's hard to comprehend how much suffering that war causes. War causes more fear on a large scale than anything else I can think of. The powers that be certainly know how to manipulate politics and create laws that cause so much chaos and fear.

Some religious types of people have many fears. Two such fears that come to mind are the fear of homosexuals, and transgender folks. The fear of transcended folks using the bathroom when girls are in the bathroom at the same time seems silly. Female restrooms in the U.S.A. have doors and provide privacy. To this day I can honestly say, I have used the public restrooms for 60 years, and have never seen anybody's private parts. The fear of Transgendered folks in general stems from the idea that anyone questioning their own sexuality, as Transgendered folks do, has to be a child molester. The fear of homosexuals is based on the idea that they are perverts and are going to try and influence your sexual preferences. There is good and bad in all people. And, to be different in the ways I have described, does not mean that you're a pervert. In fact, I have met some of the most loving people that have had to deal with the issues described above. And, isn't love what it's all about. And doesn't the bible teach tolerance. I don't concern myself with people's gender issues. It doesn't seem far-fetched to wonder if the hormones that are routinely added to our food sources might promote gender issues as well as homosexuality.

I began to wonder if the tornadoes and other bad weather that the bible belt experiences is a result of collective fear. All that negative energy in the form of judgement, fear, intolerance and hate, could be responsible for all the tornadoes and other bad weather that the bible belt experiences.

In the case of abortion, another issue that divides us. Some religious types take issue with abortion. They call themselves pro-lifers. They have a right to their beliefs. But I would tell them that chances are if a woman does not want a child, often times the unwanted child is likely to be raised without the proper amount of love to create a healthy adult, perhaps even abused, considering all the pressures that exist in the world today. If an abortion is done very early before the fertilized egg becomes a fetus, then it should be allowed and not forbidden by laws made by men.

I truly believe that some of the religious doctrines actually promote polarization. They certainly don't try and unite us in spite of our differences. They don't much promote unity and tolerance. I believe that it is a woman's right to choose. If one wants to dictate laws regarding abortion, then one should be willing to raise the child in question, or at least not be against planned parenthood. I am not opposed to aborting a fertilized egg before it becomes a fetus. That is when it is still an embryo. If god finds this offensive, then I would say that God is better at exacting justice that we are. By now I have come to the conclusion that we pay for our sins by our sins. We are constantly paying our karmic debts. Some little some big. I would say that people who regard fertilized eggs more important than a living child, is pro birth but not pro-life. They are not too concerned with the child once its born. Often times an unwanted child has no life.

It is sad that we allow policy makers to continue with policies that ensure war. We can't keep allowing policies that promote hate and fear. The problem isn't that we hate these people that are victims of wars that we are involved in. We don't even know them personally. The problem is not that we don't love these people enough to stop the insanity. We don't love them the way we should. We forget we are all one and connected. They are children of god, as we all are. The only way to show love to these folks is to stop the insanity of war. And to be awake to how the super power, (the United States) foreign policy effects the whole world, including us, since we are all connected. I often wonder why we have 800 military bases around the world. There was one president who was a four-star general, and he gave us a warning. He warned the U.S. must guard against the acquisition of unwarranted influence of military industrial complex. He said we must maintain a balance between defense spending and a healthy economy. It seems none of the leaders of the country took heed of his warning. I truly believe that our weird weather patterns are actually a reflection of our chaotic existence here on planet earth, there is no balance, and the result is an unhealthy economy.

Many religious people truly believe that they will be blessed by interfering in the middle east by supporting Israeli. "The old hippy" I mention in the chapter I labeled as **The Debate**, mentioned the Palestine issue. He said, "we will never have peace if we don't understand the Palestinian issue." Many religious people truly believe that they will be blessed by interfering in the middle east by supporting Israeli. They are just going by what they have heard, by some religious leaders and what the bible says.

After **WWII**, it was not hard for the world to feel sentiment for the Jewish people after what Hitler put them through. At that point it was easy to promote the idea of helping the Jews to create the state of Israel. Many people are influenced by the idea that god would bless those people that helped to create the state of Israeli. This idea was accomplished with the help of the United States. And we continue to interfere in the Israeli and Palestinian issue by continuing to support Israel. We give millions to Israel. In doing so it has caused anger and hate from the people that were already there for a very long time.

There are two key passages in the bible where God promises to bless those who support Israel, and to curse those who do not. The first is found in Gen. 12:2-3. The second key passage is found in Gen. 27: 29.

The bible has been used to promote this idea of helping Israel to force the Palestinians off of the land they have inhabited for hundreds of years. This idea continues to perpetuate war. People actually believe they will be cursed if they don't support this idea. Most people are so busy with the details of life that keep them so pre-occupied trying to make a living that little time or energy is left for seeking alternative beliefs, as this idea flies in the face of love and peace. They are just going by what they have heard, by some religious leaders. And the bible.

My theory is **God** is more concerned with **HOW** one lives rather than **where** one lives. In other words, how one behaves is more important than where one decides to live and misbehave. It matters more how bright one shines with the energy of light and love rather than the energy of fear that the absence of light produces.

It is hard for me to believe that god would endorse or demand any thought action or behavior that would produce anything but love. He sent his son Jesus here to teach us how to love and exist on a vibratory frequency that resonates with peace and love and healing. I believe that his vibrations are of such a frequency that he could walk on water. Jesus said blessed are the peacemaker for they shall be called the children of God.

Jesus said that wherever two or more are gathered in my name there HE shall be also. So, it doesn't matter where people gather to live. It matters more how one behaves where ever they are gathered. There is a lot of territory on this planet that could be inhabited by those who take the high road. **Imagine all the people sharing all the world.** I don't think god would be concerned where the people live as long as they live in peace. And I have heard it said, "where ever you go, there you are." So, it does not matter where you live, there you are. Make it a peaceful existence. Peace comes from within don't seek it without. Isn't it weird that the powerful peace makers of the world are all dead? The really powerful ones that could and did help to elevate world consciousness. They helped to raise the vibrations of the world. And they were killed.

The major religions that have been involved in wars throughout history obviously take their cue from their particular religious doctrines. I believe in the idea that the temple of god is within, like Jesus said. That is to say god is within all of us. And, we were made in the image and likeness of him. My thoughts are that god is love or the energy of love, since we are made up of energy. God dwells within us as the energy of love. We are made in his image and likeness. He is Divine energy. We are part of the trinity **of love, light, and energy**. Our energy is our **spirit.** The energy part never dies, (only changes form- physics law) because the spirit lives on. The spirit is the part of us that never dies. God is the light. And, we are starlight. God is love or the vibration of love in the form of compassionate thoughts or emotions.

We express god when our thoughts are free of judgement and fear. And our behavior follows. Keeping our thought forms pure and free of judgement requires work though. I find myself asking the great spirit, or my higher-self to help me adhere to these beliefs. It is not always easy in today's world. Prayer or meditation is important to help us keep our thought forms pure. If we don't like how things are, we have to change the way we think and feel about a situation and the situation will change. A wise man said if you "change the way you think of things and the things you think of will change." In my meditation I ask the great spirit (god, my higher self) to help me adhere to this idea of keeping my thought forms pure and free of judgement, grant me the help it takes to remain non-judgmental and free of fear.

I think that Jesus wanted to teach us to love and forgive. Somewhere along the line that information has been altered from its original message, of love and forgiveness. The alteration of the original message has allowed and endorsed war and torture and man's inhumanity to man in the name of god for a long time. I believe the alteration was implemented by design at the **council of Nicea**. It was a council of Christian bishops. It took place about 325 A D, it was then that it was decided by religious leaders, which books were scripture and which were burned. Thanks to the notorious habit of early Christian leaders, we may never know what books/scrolls, existed before the council of Nicea.

The idea of keeping feminine energy down by the defamation of feminine energy certainly has taken hold even today as many religious doctrines reflect this mind set. I see legislation being enacted as I write this, that take away a woman's right to terminate a pregnancy, in as much as planned parenthood is being defunded by men in government. It's sad because planned parenthood also makes contraceptives available, as well as pelvic exams that can often determine health issues such as abnormal cell growth within the uterus. Planned parenthood made it affordable for women to have choices with regard to their own bodies. It seems ludicrous that men in high places can enact laws regarding women's bodies.

It seems there is diabolical plan to keep women in a place that is at the very least less comfortable than men. I think this is done to keep women from having a true input on changing the world in a positive way.

I was reminded by my eldest grandson, while in deep conversation with him that **Democracy**, is the idea that everyone should have a quality of life. Democracy is for the common good. And I would have to tell religious leaders who live in opulence and preach benevolence that they should set an example. Be the change you wish to see here. See to it that everyone is taken care of, and not just you. **" Shoe the children with no shoes on their feet house the people living in the street. Oh oh there's a solution**. Those lyrics resonate with me as I remember the song fly like an eagle by Stevie Miller band.

I think that religious doctrines that prohibit birth control, are ludicrous. We are under the strong influence of the powers that be, and we know how they love to withhold money and cause misery. And they don't like sharing. They feed off of our struggle to survive. I come from a large Hispanic family, and my devoutly religious aunties who followed religious doctrines which prohibited birth control (except for the rhythm method), ended up having 10 children. I saw some of them struggle to provide for their large families. And it's an unnatural struggle. The stress of making money is causing distress and disease. People have always worked hard throughout history in an effort to survive. And it seems that throughout history there is always a form of government that takes from the poor and allows the powerful to live in opulence, including religious establishments that are free from paying taxes, they have many vulgar displays of wealth while the serfs perform the work. I am reminded of Louie the sixteenth and Marie Antionette. They both were beheaded for displaying vulgar displays of wealth while the commonwealth was starving.

CHAPTER 27

ARE WE ASLEEP?

I believe that if people were fully awake, they would be outraged. I'm writing this book in an effort to wake people up. Most people are good law-abiding people. We are empathetic and compassionate for the most part. Having said that, I would think that we would be gravitating towards leaders who would prioritize peace and be working towards peaceful solutions. I think there must be a collective component to the solution.

We are not promoting peace and love if we allow hawks to run our government. We have to open our eyes and see the powers that be for who they truly are. Warmongers who seldom go to war themselves but they create wars for our children to fight and die. It seems the United States military is always flexing its muscle somewhere.

Most people consider themselves to be good human beings. And they truly are. As a matter of fact, they are children of god as we all are. And the temple of god lies within, within all of us. The problem is many people are asleep. I actually think there is a diabolical plan to keep us asleep and to keep us in fear. I have heard for years that the fluoride that is put in the water is not good for us. They say it is part of a plan to dummy us down. And in fact, fluoride is believed to cover the third eye. The third eye is the reference given to the pineal gland. And is associated with enlightenment. And in my studies, I learned that the jewel that the Hindu women wear in the middle of their foreheads is symbolic of their third eye being open, or being enlightened. And thus the **11:11 awakening code**, it is time for the people who have been asleep to wake up. **I'm reminded of another song from back in the day by Pink Floyd. It's called Comfortably numb. These words resonate with me, "Have WE become comfortably numb."**

We can't be fully awake if we are so comfortable in our little world that we ignore global issues. If people follow along like sheeple, then yes, there will always be war. We have to quit being **sheeple.** I believe that the powers that be have manipulated information throughout history. Many religions endorse doctrines that are intended to perpetuate war forever. I think we should be aware of that fact, so that we are more likely to question ideas put forth by the powers that be, as well as some religious doctrines, then we will be more likely to promote the idea of peace and question the idea of war. Jesus said blessed are the peace makers for they shall be called the children of **god.**

CHAPTER 28

THE PEACE AND LOVE GENERATION

So many of the songs of the 60's and 70's came from a place of love and peace and passion with regard to protesting war and the status quo. I often think about how the Native Americans understood this idea that we are all **one**. They were all about the circle of life. And, they knew that we were all connected. The Native Americans may have fought battles for food stores if times were hard, but they never fought wars over some deep dark political objective. It became obvious to me that there is a link between the more peaceful Native American tribes, and the hippies who were so opposed to war and promoted peace and love, and respect for all that is natural, including mother earth. There is a common thread between Native Americans and the Hippy's. In both cases, mind altering plants, like marijuana and peyote, and other psychedelic drugs were used. I believe that natural occurring mind-altering plants, when used in a spiritual manner have been instrumental in gaining spiritual enlightenment. These plants were instrumental in native culture and gave them insight to the idea that we are all connected and the fact that everything was sacred to them.

I know of several very educated young new age hippies that travel to Peru to do these plants, under the supervision of Incan shaman, to gain spiritual enlightenment.

There were lots of war protests taking place in the 60's and 70's. As it turned out that war ended. But not without much opposition from the powers that be as evidenced by Kent State University. The National Guard opened fire killing peaceful (unarmed) students protesting the war. How dare they question the deep dark political objective of the powers that be. I bring these things up because we don't need to be forgetting these things. It's as though there is this deep dark political force or machine that just has to have war. And the hippies and lots of others stood up to the war machine.

If you get enough energy (collective thoughts, emotions, and feelings) you can make changes. I think it was 6 months after the song (Eve of Destruction) that the draft ended. The words and the passion demonstrated in the song, was instrumental in getting rid of the draft. Words like "Old enough to kill but not for voting, you don't believe in war but what's that gun your totin'." And, the music of the 60' and 70's depicted the consciousness of the young people at the time and their opposition to war.

I graduated from high school in 1968, and the Viet- Nam war was raging on. I remember many of my young male friends having long hair, and looking forward to enjoying life after graduation. We were enjoying our youth and experiencing the amazing energy that permeated the atmosphere at that time. Jesus freaks on every corner. Peace and love abounding from so many sources. So many songs permeated our minds and hearts and souls. The words to the song 'Imagine all the people living life as One' comes to mind as supporting the spiritual concept of oneness.

There are many ways that the powers that be distract us from the issues that plague us as a people of planet earth. If we are not the type of people that are likely to break the law by using street drugs, that's not a problem. There are numerous pharmaceuticals available that are legal, but cause just as much chaos and pain as the street drugs. We have numerous prescription drugs available, that were introduced by the powers that be. Oh yes whatever the issue, there is a drug to make you feel better for a minute. Big pharma has that one covered. Oh, but be careful because the powers that be have designed laws that will put you in jail if you fall into the trap of self-medicating to ease the pain of our struggle to survive in a sick world. I read a joke where the doctor tells the patient take this prescription and don't worry if the drug doesn't address the issue because the side effect, are far worse than the original issue, and you are sure to forget about the original issue.

There are so many ways we self-medicate in an effort to ease the struggle of surviving in a chaotic world. However, there is sure to be a law to get us in trouble if we do take advantage of the alcohol or illicit drugs that are available. How ironic that we can drive to a bar conveniently located throughout the city. But don't get caught leaving that bar with alcohol in your system. It's as if they set you up. It's also crazy that alcohol has been legal and it's a struggle to legalize weed which is proven to be good medicine. I can see why the powers that be would not want us smoking the peace pipe loaded with pot. Smoke pot and the last thing you want to do is fight. It's hard for the powers that be to get their war on if people are smoking the peace pipe. We saw much opposition to war in the peace and love generation.

I have read that the powers that be began introducing hard drugs into places that were heavily populated by the hippies. For example, I have watched documentaries that suggest that the hard drugs were introduced to Haight Ashbury by the powers that be. Haight Ashbury is referred to as the origin of the hippy counterculture. My thoughts are that the powers that be are responsible for introducing hard drugs into Haight, so that young people would become addicted to the very harmful and addictive drugs like cocaine and heroin. In this way they were able to defamate the hippy movement. In this way they were able to distract the hippies from their enlightened path of peace and love.

There was a stream of consciousness that flowed from Laurel Canyon, located in the Hollywood hills region of the Santa Monica mountains. This seemed to be a hub for several young musical artists. These artists songs were mildly political and expressed a cross breeding of folk and psychedelic rock, and some of the greatest music ever written came from there. Laurel Canyon was a "shangrila" for many artists and was the beginning of bands such as The Eagles, Crosby Stills Nash and Young, Joni Mitchell, Frank Zappa, Jim Morrison of The Doors. Michelle Phillips and John Phillips of The Mamas and Papas, just to name a few. Many of them took drugs together and created some of the best music ever made.

I have always thought marijuana should be referred to as an herb rather than a drug. It should not be in the same category as heroin and cocaine and other hard drugs. It is a powerful healing herb not a destructive drug. The worse thing that can happen is a person acquires an appetite. This works well for people undergoing chemotherapy, because they tend to lose their appetite for nutrition. I must say I have known people that should not smoke the herb until their work is done because it can relax a person so much that they become unmotivated. However, the vast majority of folks that I know, who smoke the herb are motivated. That would include myself. In fact, in Spanish the herb is often referred to as mota, and me and other people I know call it mota vation. I certainly don't want pharmaceutical drugs to once again be the only choice for many health related issues, I don't think people that have hard drug issues including alcoholism should be punished, but rather it may be cheaper, and more humane to rehabilitate.

And I would like to bolster all those statements regarding Native American intuitiveness, by interjecting my own experiences as a hippie and the psychedelic black sheep of my family. I say that in jest. I have always felt loved by my family but I have never been truly understood by some of them. It has given me a different perspective, and I believe that the psychedelic drugs when used in a spiritual manner can actually promote opening of the third eye. And my personal experience with magic mushrooms (psilocybin) allowed me to see the trees breathing. It allowed me to actually see energy and how people are connected and that there is no place where you end and I begin, we are all this soup of energy. And having seen the trees breathe and knowing that they are alive, I am drawn to hug them, and do when I have the opportunity. Another song of the peace and love generation, comes to mind It's called "Dragging The Line." by Tommy James, I chose these random words, the words go something like this

"Dragging the line"

making a living the old hard way
taking and giving my day by day
I feel fine I'm talking about
peace of mind
Loving the free and feeling spirit
of hugging a tree when you get near it.

At this point I would like to interject with the spiritual concept that employs the idea that if we all lived our lives with loving thoughts instead of fear that we would collectively create an experience, we could refer to as paradise. In other words, if our thoughts create our reality as **quantum physics** suggests, and if our collective thoughts were always free of negative energy, then collectively, we would create a reality based on love (paradise) not fear which can be hell on earth. This idea depicted in the temple of the descending gods, by one of the two pillars. A reality that we would rather avoid, so that is why it is important for us to have our thought forms purified so that we have positive thoughts. This in an effort to create the other reality, one based on love, where everyone is happy (paradise). As we all know it's very difficult in today's society to stay positive all the time, especially when certain events take place that tend to bring fearful thoughts. There are so many hurdles that so many of us have to climb in an effort to survive and achieve peace and happiness.

Personally, I don't think that god would want anything but "peace and good brotherhood." Having said that I'm reminded of another spiritual song of that hippy era. These random lines from the song are examples of enlightenment.

Crystal blue persuasion
(random lines)

better get ready
to see the light

maybe tomorrow
when he looks down
there will be peace
and good brotherhood
crystal blue persuasion

Another good example of songs that nailed the issue is called "we have been asking questions."

How did it happen,
How were we played
for fools
Gambling with our children's
lives in a game that knows
No rules. We need an answer
A reason why, the rulers wage the wars
And our children fight n die

I think I know how it happened. The introduction of money religion and technology. Yes, my friends we have been played for fouls. That statement reminds me of a song by The Who. The words were **"We won't be fooled again."** Well we have been fooled again and again.

Perhaps the laws that enslave us and cause turmoil in our lives is another way the powers that be keep us from living more peaceful and harmonious lives. I say this because, in the 60's and 70's many young folks woke up to this conspiracy. I have known for a long time that the powers that be don't want to legalize pot. It is the medicine that helped so many people wake up. It helps with medical issues and mental issues as well. My favorite doctor and guru from India readily asserted that cannabis and other mind altering plants have a legitimate place in spirituality and medicine. He asserted this while being interviewed by high times. Cannabis is a very benign way of helping humanity deal with the insanity of the current world we are experiencing on planet earth school. It defiantly promotes peace.

My thoughts are that every state should legalize the medicine (pot). I say this because the legalization of pot in the state of Colorado has led to the influx of thousands of folks moving here with sick children who have seizures, and other ailments such as M.S. and cancer. These ailments have been treated successfully with cannabis. And there are some folks that just like being high or under the influence of marijuana. There are those folks that like smoking the herb and have moved here in an effort to no longer be criminals. They can come out of the closet here in Colorado. In any case it has driven up housing prices and has flooded our freeways to a point that it causes stress for many people on any given day.

CHAPTER 29

THE 1% SECRET SOCIETIES

Some folks, including myself, believe that, it is a diabolical plan by **the secret societies**. To keep us preoccupied with such things as making a living that there is little time or energy to spend on seeking truth or questioning the status quo. They are so good at creating distractions. We have cell phones. We have video games. We have the national pastime of football, and other sports. Then there is overeating, another pastime that serves to numb us temporarily. Perhaps, we have become comfortably numb. There are any number of neurotic responses to the crazy world we live in. And these preoccupations certainly serve to take the people's minds off of the current problems that plague the whole planet. I would remind people that even if we distract ourselves with various pastimes', the negative energy is still ever-present.

There is a breaking point when people have had enough, and we are beginning to reach that threshold. As I write this, there are demonstrations going on all over the country. People, especially young people who are concerned with the planet. They are tired of mother earth being exploited. They are no longer accepting war as the status quo. As more and more people are experiencing the awakening code, the more conscious people are becoming, the more of this energy is added to the collective. Every human being has the code within them. I believe the code is being activated in more and more people. I read that there is a direct relationship between our chakras being activated and enlightenment. In other words, the more enlightened we become, the more activated our chakras become the more the code is being uncovered, and more people are experiencing the 11 11 awakening code. Now that we are in the age of Aquarius, more and more veils are being removed.

I listened to a speech from my favorite all time president, who was assassinated in 1963. In this speech he refers to the secret societies. It is referred to as the speech that killed him. He starts out by saying that the very word **secrecy** is repugnant to a free and open society. He states that we are as a people, inherently and historically opposed to secret societies, secret oaths and secret proceedings. His intentions were clearly to expose and put an end to them. However, as it turned out they put an end to him. In that speech he asks for the peoples help to expose and put an end to the secrecy. He goes on to say we are opposed to a monolithic, ruthless conspiracy that relies primarily on **covet** means for expanding its sphere of influence. The speech is defiantly worth listening to.

I don't think his speech made much sense to many people at the time. However, as time has gone on, and life has unfolded, to expose the secret societies, and the fact that they have control over our entire lives. The ruthlessness as described by my favorite president is dictating that we are no longer just coveting material items, we are now yearning for clean water, a peaceful world, healthy food free of pesticides, more money to ease the stress of life. Etc..

The word **covet** means to yearn for something. The meaning goes straight to my point regarding people's desire for material goods. Most material items don't last and end up in the landfills. Some fall in the category of hazardous materials. I saw it unfolding in the 50's as all the consumer items were being unleashed upon the unsuspecting consumer population.

The hostess man unfolding his 3-tiered array of hostess goodies upon our front porch. I remember mom purchasing an aluminum air tight canister set. A set of knives, a vacuum, oh, and the Fuller brush, the man had a wonderful display. Then we had to have a new car. Then mom had to go to work. Then dad took to drinking. It seemed that the ripple effect of the insertion of material items for us to covet had a very negative effect on our young lives as children our family life took a blow. Once mom got a job our entire lives changed. She then tried to compensate by giving us material things, but we much preferred to have her love by way of her time and attention.

The insertion of all the consumer items that are available for people to yearn for or covet are vast. This yearning creates an environment whereby people's desires for material items, drive them to seek ways to make money to have material items which they believe will make them happier. This desire creates the environment where people become creative in their ways of attaining the items they seek. Greed is a monster that is being expressed every day. One way it manifests itself by exploitation. It allows business folks to take advantage of skilled labor or even unskilled labor.

It then becomes a situation whereby business people hire skilled laborers to do what they themselves cannot do. My life experience with working for co-operations have supported this idea of enslavement. It has been my experience as a skilled laborer, that many skills have been exploited. For example, as a massage therapist, I found myself working for corporations. In most cases the owners do not have the license or skills or schooling to be therapists.

However, they are business people, and they take the lion's share that the consumer pays for the cost of a massage. It then makes it hard for a small business owner to compete with the corporations. I found the same situation regarding the hair cutting business. I hold licenses in both fields and have seen lots of exploitation over the years. It does sting a little when you see the owners driving around in very expensive cars and you can't afford tires.

I often wonder how the top 1% percent of the population that hold most of the wealth can sleep at night, knowing there are so many folks doing without the basic things that allow for some quality of life. It's as if they have no human feelings at all. Perhaps they **are not** human at all. The super-rich **(top 1%)** could literally throw millions in the toilet without missing it. If they had human qualities like compassion, and love of their fellow man they could not enjoy their level of comfort without feeling as though they should contribute to the welfare of mankind. I do not believe there are very many **humans** that would not display compassion for their fellow man, if they knew he was hungry or cold or visibly suffering if it was in their realm of possibilities to help. Of course, there are sick humans that inflict pain on others, but I can guarantee that they were abused themselves. However, the average person that was raised with any love at all are sensitive to the suffering of others. Most people are compassionate.

The powers that be keep us in fear and so busy trying to make a living, and in many cases struggling to do so. If we are busy, then we have no time to wonder why things are the way they are. We have been conditioned to be good people (sheeple). And they are the sheep herders. We just go along like sheeple and question nothing. We are just happy to have a couple days off every week, to be with family, to relax and recuperate from the hassles of the work week.

That would include for many, the drive to and from work, (traffic). And the stress of making ends meet. People just want to relax on their days off and rest and have enough left over on their checks to do something enjoyable even if it's just to buy a six pack, or a little herb to help them relax and unwind. They are happy to have some rest till Monday comes along and start all over again. Sadly, there are many folks that never even get a day off, working two jobs does not allow it.

The powers that be seem to be devoid of all the qualities that are innate in human beings. How can super rich beings live in opulence and have so many vulgar displays of wealth while some people are starving and have no place to lay their heads at night. Every human being deserves a nest, a place to lay their head at night and rest peacefully. I believe it is no measure of health to be well adjusted to a sick society. This statement is a reflection on our society as a whole. We are led in the wrong direction by the powers that be. My thoughts are if you find yourself having more than you need, you don't build walls you increase the size of your table.

The opposite of love is fear. The powers that be are very good at keeping people in fear. Many people wonder where their next meal is coming from or if it's coming. These kinds of thoughts can invoke some fearful thoughts. There is fear involved in not knowing if I can pay rent. Or, wondering if my family will have a roof over its head next week. Those fearful thoughts can't even compare to the thoughts that must go through the heads of folks who live under constant conditions of war.

We are beginning to reach threshold. As I write this there are demonstrations going on all over the country. People, especially young people who are concerned with the planet. They are tired of mother earth being exploited. They are no longer accepting war as the status quo. As more and more people are experiencing the awakening code, the more consciences people are becoming. Every human being has the code within them. I believe the code is being activated in more and more people. I read that there is a direct relationship between our chakras being activated and enlightenment. In other words, the more enlightened we become, the more activated our chakras are. The more the code is being uncovered, is a reflection of more people who are experiencing the 11 11 awakening code. Now that we are in the age of Aquarius, the more the veils are being removed.

There is a very diabolical force on this planet, that is so profound and pervasive its intention is to spread its warlike tentacles over the entire planet. This diabolical force uses religion as a tool to make sure the energy of war exists. This force invades every aspect of our lives. **President Eisenhower** warned of the military industrial complex taking over. I believe he was a four-star general and knew the atrocities of war. Personally, I don't think anyone who has not been to war should be able to make war happen with political decisions.

The powers that be use money religion and technology as their weapon of choice. Our weapon of choice must be our collective spirituality. Those lines are in my poem at the back of the book.

CHAPTER 30

TREATMENT OF ANIMALS

Our treatment of animals, in the case of factory farming, is another example of fear on a large scale. What could be worse than spending your whole life in a miserable situation knowing the whole time that the day will come that you will be butchered. The cattle stand in the mud and their own feces, they live in miserable conditions all their lives. Our treatment of many animals that we use for food is another example of fear being unleashed. The treatment of factory farmed animals is sad. Yet it goes on every day. And it's sad that many chickens are kept in the dark all their lives. I know it's difficult to address these issues, but it's not impossible. I bring this up because of the fear and misery that these animals go through is immeasurable. Remember, we are eating that energy. I am referring to the physics law that states "energy can-not be created or destroyed, just change form." So, if we eat the flesh from the animals that have suffered, we will be affected by that meat that we eat. It is no wonder that there are so many ailments in today's world.

We should be aware that raising livestock for food puts out an incredible amount of methane gas. This gas is very harmful to the ozone layer. I think that energy should be exerted in the direction of finding solutions. If we are not part of the solution, then we are part of the problem. We must be more conscious on a collective level regarding our choices. If we choose to eat animals then we must make sure that animals are treated with kindness, and under humane conditions until the time comes to end the life of the animals. At some point we need to reject the inhumane treatment of animals to quench our desire for animal flesh. Free range is a good choice for those of us who can't break away from eating animals.

Those of us who do love meat should certainly try to buy meat that is free range and grass fed. A happy cow. Remember, you will take on that energy. There were times when I have eaten meat from animals that have suffered. I can honestly say that my injured back will bother me more after eating animals that have suffered. I learned to avoid eating animals that have suffered. And now, I no longer allow myself to eat meat. I believe that free range and grass-fed cows are happier. Raising animals in feed lots is not good for the ozone as the animals give off methane gas. Methane emitted from the livestock sector contributes to greenhouse gas emissions worldwide.

Man has notoriously subjected animals to such misery for our amusement as well as for the bottom line. Grow them quick. Add hormones to help it along. There is something the Hispanics refer to as pork dreams. And many of them love to eat pork chili, and often times one will experience those pork dreams after eating a bowl or two of that delicious pork chili. You can't have just one bowl, and with that second bowl you need another tortilla and then you still have a little tortilla left then you need a little more chili and at this point it's a cycle. Hence pork dreams. More like pork nightmares. The negative energy is taken on by the eater and that energy comes out in the dreams.

I like the way some Native Americans tribes approached the idea of food. They followed the buffalo, they did not feel the need to fence and brand. How cruel to burn a brand into the cow. How painful is that? And they used every part of the animal. And they gave the animal honor and respect by wearing the hide and displayed the horns etc. in the most ornamental ways.

CHAPTER 31

MESA VERDE / THE CLIFF DWELLINGS

Irecently had occasion to visit the cliff dwellings of Mesa Verde National Park. It is believed that the people began living in the pueblos they built beneath the overhanging cliffs around the 1190's. The structures included villages of more than 150 rooms. They continued residing in alcoves and constructing new rooms for 100 years. It is believed that the population began migrating south into present day New Mexico, and Arizona. By 1300's the occupation of the cliff dwellings ended.

I took photos of the pictures that were on display at the park. I found some of the photos to be quite interesting. I have to believe that the natives of the cliff dwellings were visited by ancient aliens. I say this because of the photo resembling the most basic sacred geometric design, the spiral. The spiral is clearly depicted in the photo. And the fact that the spiral is connected to the smaller spiral is an indication that these primitive people had an understanding of sacred geometry and our connection to the cosmos. Nikola Tesla said that "we are to the universe as a wave is to the ocean." PART OF THE WHOLE. We are all connected. The spiral is duplicated in the galaxies, our DNA, (double helix) the twisting of a tornado, the way water runs down the drain, the spiral shape of the crowns in our heads, etc....

The concept was first described in the Emerald Tablets of Hermes Trismegistus: that which is below corresponds to that which is above. It is said that we are a microcosm of the macrocosm. We are part of the universal mind. That Divine mind that we can tap into when using the pendulum.

I found the photo that resembles waves to be interesting to me as well. Consciousness is the ability to be aware of one's self and ones surroundings In other words to take in information. We take in information through our 5 senses. The brain then decodes the information into our reality. For example, the reason we hear music or language when someone is speaking to us is because the information comes to us by way of vibrational sound waves. The sound wave hits the ear drum and parts of the inner ear hammer out the wave according to its vibration. You can't see the waves because they are invisible vibrational waves. The same with smell we can't see the waves but our brain receives the waves by way of the olfactory nerve and the brain then decodes the information into our reality. I am reminded of the Bible verse that says "In the beginning was the WORD, and the word was with god and the word was god. John 1:1. The word is vibration. Nikola Tesla said "if you wish to understand the universe, think energy, frequency and vibration." Perhaps the natives did have an understanding of this concept and perhaps it was ancient aliens who imparted this knowledge to the natives.

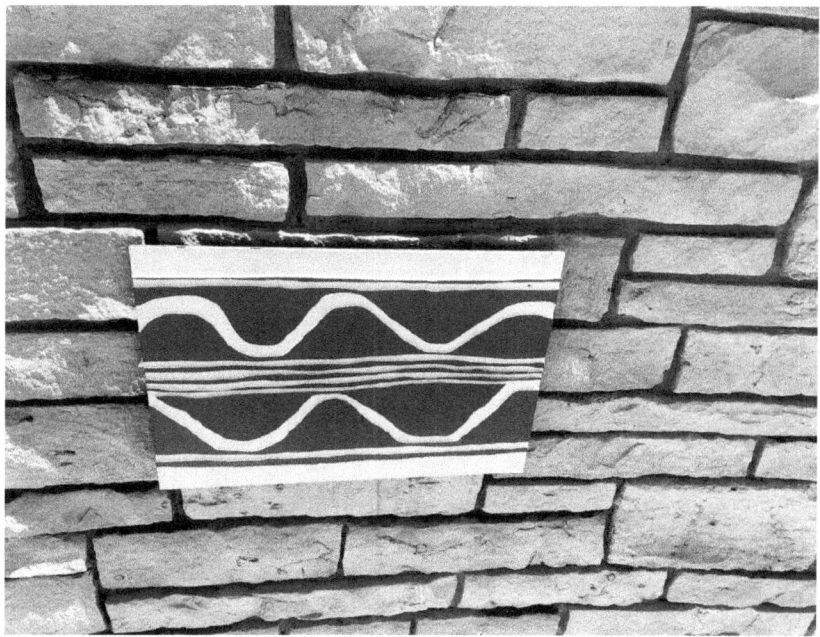

CHAPTER 32

SUPPRESSION OF FEMININE ENERGY

Women have made a lot of headway in the past 75 years with regard to women's rights, and it's time we use our feminine energy to influence political decisions. I have always thought that if women would be allowed more of a political input there would be less war. Female energy is needed to provide the balance to male energy. Both energies are necessary. In a more natural setting, male energy is needed to protect the family from harm, to hunt, to provide etc... Not many women would knowingly promote war knowing that her son would likely be a soldier in that war. No mother wants to send her son to war especially if it can be avoided.

A long time ago there was a council (council of Nicaea) and it was decided what parts of the bible would be shared and used by the masses. It involved promoting parts of the bible that involve defamation of females and promotes keeping feminine energy down. For example, I believe that Jesus did have a significant other and her name was Mary Magdalene. I have heard her referred to as a whore. And, I remember learning that Eve tempted Adam. Blame it on the women. In this way it's easy to continue the defamation of the sacred feminine. Eventually the attitude took hold and women are trying to catch up ever since. The middle east has a whole lot of catching up to do.

In my parents' lifetime women had to fight for the right to vote. I remember attending weddings and the vows that many people took. A woman frequently repeated the vow to love, honor, cherish and **obey** her husband. And, I remember watching on television that at one time women were not allowed to express their opinion with regard to politics or other important matters. If they did, they were paraded around town with a bit in their mouth and subject to public humiliation. And heaven forbid, if she were a natural healer like a reiki, practitioner who used natural healing methods, to help with sickness. She would then be labeled a witch and tortured by certain religious types.

The Spanish inquisition is a perfect example. In these cases, women were tortured, and called witches. Often times burned at the stake. And, the binding of women's feet in the orient. This was done to girls so their feet would be small, however it caused pain and deformity. And this was done to be more pleasing to a man. Torture a girl child all her life so she can be pleasing to a man. This method of binding was painful and did not allow for a girl child to play like normal children. You can't make this stuff up.

Those are some examples of feminine energy being stifled, making men more important than women. It occurred to me that in the middle east, where feminine energy is suppressed there is more violence. And from the pictures I have seen of countries like that, they seem to be devoid of the beauty and creativity that feminine energy brings forth. I then got a picture in my mind of how colorful and artful cultures such as the native Americans were. They had more balance of energies. Men spent their entire time honing their skills to provide for the families within the tribe.

It seems there is diabolical plan to keep women in a place that is at the very least less comfortable than men. I think this is done to keep women from having a true input on changing the world in a positive way.

Keeping feminine energy down is another way of promoting imbalance of energies and perpetuating war. The powers that be have known that not many women would knowingly promote war knowing that her son would likely be a soldier in that war. No mother wants to send her son to war especially if it can be avoided.

The idea of keeping feminine energy down certainly has taken hold even today as many religious doctrines reflect this mind set. I see legislation being enacted as I write this, that take away a woman's right to terminate a pregnancy, in as much as planned parenthood is being defunded by men in government. It's sad because planned parenthood also makes contraceptives available, as well as pelvic exams that can often determine health issues such as abnormal cell growth within the uterus. Planned parenthood made it affordable for women to have choices with regard to their own bodies. It seems ludicrous that men in high places can enact laws regarding women's bodies. Most importantly it made available contraceptives, in this way it would prevent unwanted pregnancies.

As I mentioned before, keeping feminine energy suppressed, is instrumental in achieving the goal of contributing to never ending war. And, it doesn't take a rocket scientist to see that the alterations are in fact doing the job that they were designed to do. Religious wars have been occurring throughout history and continue to this day. One way of keeping feminine energy down was the way women were targeted if they were considered witches. Burning people alive wasn't unusual, as well as other forms of torture. If religious doctrine was questioned, then one was deemed **a heretic**, and you know the story they were not treated well.

I am sure some of the women referred to as witches were actually healers who employed the use of the herb marijuana. I am sure these women used the herb for its medicinal properties. Perhaps they used it themselves and their third eye was opened and privy to the secrets that are revealed to many people who use the herb and other mind-altering spiritual earth drugs that promoted enlightenment. And once enlightened, they became a threat to the status quo. Often times it was religious folks that carried out the torment that these accused women were forced to undergo. And I know the use of the herb helps to wake you up, and once awake your soul demands you question the status quo.

I often wonder why we were taught to fear witches and not the people that burned them alive. As a Reiki practitioner, I have seen many healings done as a result of passing on the energy of the herb. The use of the herb combined with meditation can be instrumental in the process of opening the **third eye**, and allows one to vibrate at a higher frequency and promotes the healing of others, and allows you to live a more peaceful existence. And I'm pretty sure that my ability to help promote healing has something to do with the frequency at which I vibrate. There are many people whom I have treated who would never smoke marijuana, but they enjoy the healing energy of the herb, that is being passed on to them through energy work like reike and reflexology. I would like to say that I think all women have this ability to help with the healing process. Women are natural healers and nurturers under ideal circumstances. That is why I believe that feminine energy has been stifled.

Every culture has their healers. In the Hispanic world natural healers are called curanderas. There was a time that these particular women were well respected as healers. Long before big pharma came along. And, it doesn't take much stretch of the imagination to know that those women probably employed the use of marijuana in their repertoire of herbal medicine. Hispanic people have long been victims of laws that were passed to punish marijuana users. Propaganda, like refer madness was used to demonize the idea of marijuana use. The population is becoming more educated with regard to natural healing, and the use of the herb marijuana is becoming more accepted as people are becoming more educated. The laws are becoming more lenient in some states, with regard to marijuana as people become more educated to the fact that marijuana is a very powerful herb for healing. And the more folks smoke the herb the more they wake up.

Smoke pot and the last thing you want to do is fight. It's hard for the powers that be to get their war on if people are smoking the peace pipe. We saw much opposition to war in the peace and love generation.

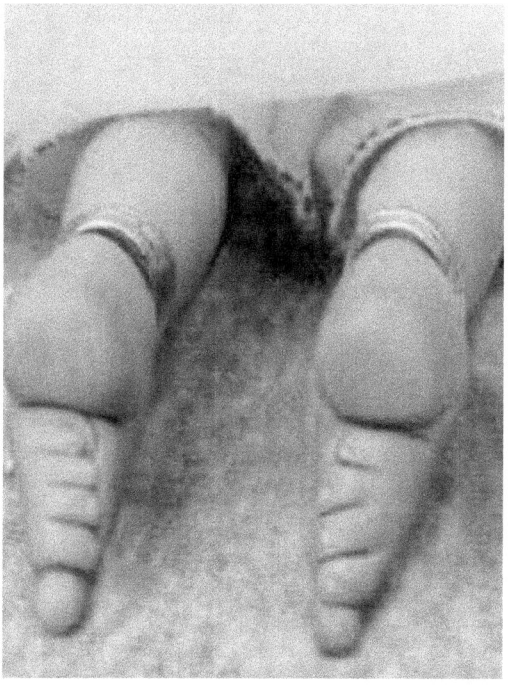

Photo taken from World Shocking History at
https://www.facebook.com/WorldShockingHistory/

This is a photo of a woman's feet being bound in childhood in the orient. This was done in effort to be more pleasing to man. Small feet were used to be more attractive and pleasing to men.

CHAPTER 33

ANCIENT ALIENS

I recently watched a documentary on ancient aliens. The documentary was pointing out that within Da Vinci's works of art were hidden symbols. I found it very interesting that it was pointed out that hidden within the Mona Lisa was a picture of an alien. And I have heard it suggested that perhaps Leonardo Da Vinci as well as others considered to be geniuses actually had help from aliens. In any case, the fact that the alien face can be seen in that famous painting makes a case for the idea that Da Vinci and others, were perhaps schooled by aliens, and perhaps were privy to lots of information (with alien help) that may have contributed to their genius. However, since this information was not to be shared by the masses, it had to be hidden within the artwork.

NASA sent a probe to Mars and the government did not tell us that there was a pyramid and sphinx on Mars. Take note of this, Mars is considered the home base of Aries, Aries means war god in Greek. And the **Arian** race were said to be seeded by these Extraterrestrial beings. In other words, if this is true, then there are monsters walking among us that look very human but have no heart or soul. Monsters like Hitler and his henchmen. And there are monsters that can sleep at night knowing that they could never spend the money that they have amassed in numerous lifetimes. Yet, they continue to withhold money that could alleviate the struggle that so many folks around the world are experiencing. I would like to point out that the bible makes a case for aliens in the old testament. I believe the fallen angels were said to have mated the female humans.

The pyramid is the symbol of the elite. The pyramid is on our dollar bill. In God we trust. I think that perhaps it's a symbol of the idea that the powers that be have succeeded in making money our god. The separation of the all seeing eye, from the rest of the pyramid, that's on the dollar bill is an indication of the idea that there is an **us** and a **them**. The money lovers, and us.

I once read that aliens have genetically altered the human race, split our DNA apart (double helix). They did this in an effort to control us as a human race by making us forget who we are. We forget we are stardust. And we are all part of god. I read that as we become more enlightened, as more veils are lifted, as vibrations are raised individually and ultimately collective that our chakras are simultaneously being activated. The awakening code is in our DNA. we are starting to remember who we are. We are remembering that we are starlight, we are all divine beings. And we are all connected. We are to the universe as a wave is to the ocean.

Jesus said that we are created in his image and likeness. He also said greater things shall you do than I have done, in my name. God is LOVE. And, if we make a collective effort on behalf of love, and reach a critical mass, we can then bring about peace. Perhaps Jesus was referring to the idea, that we on a collective level are as powerful as he was and we are capable of changing the future with our collective thoughts of love. Jesus said "Wherever three or more are gathered there I shall be also." We are capable of using our collective energy of love to change the future if enough of us are awake and questioning the status quo. Once we wake up to the idea that money was introduced to separate us. People chase money, and it leads to the haves and the have nots, and the have mores. In other words, it leads to separation. How clever the diabolical ones are. They know how to work us.

They know that united we stand divided we fall. And, numerous religions throughout history have been killing one another in the name of god. They feed off of negative energy. Einstein said, "Everything is energy, and that's all there is." We self-actualize when we enjoy the positive energy of love. It seems that the cards are stacked against us by design.

It is plain to see the root of all evil is the love of money. Money has become more important than the human race. And I say that money was introduced and continues to exist because it provides the atmosphere where by greed can be expressed. And greed obviously causes so much pain for so many. I think that the superrich could literally throw billions in the toilet and never miss it. I think that it's not the **acquisition** of money for the superrich, the 1%, that feeds their ego or feeds their desire to have power. Rather **withholding** from us (the masses) that creates the energy that these beings need. I'm talking the 1% that hold most of the wealth.

The powers that be need for us to be at odds with each other, they need to divide us. For they know that united we stand divided we fall. They enact tax laws that put a burden on the folks that make decent money. Then they can't enjoy their hard-earned money to the fullest extent. And this puts them at odds with the folks that are in need of public assistance. Many folks resent people that are on public assistance. Especially those who have received welfare for 2 or 3 generations. I would like to remind these people who are resentful that these folks on welfare that they stimulate the economy in there way too. They have to buy products like anyone else. And I think some cycles are hard to break. I wouldn't want to walk a mile in their shoes. I am grateful that my life's lessons have taught me to be a hard worker. We all have different lessons and different paths. This situation causes resentment from the folks that went to school and worked hard to acquire a level of comfort they desire. Meanwhile the billionaires and super rich get out of paying taxes by making sure tax laws favor them.

The major religions that have been involved in wars throughout history obviously take their que from their particular religious doctrines. I believe in the idea that the temple of god is within, like Jesus said. That is to say god is within all of us. And, we were made in the image and likeness of him. My thoughts are that god is love or the energy of love, since we are made up of energy. God dwells within us as the energy of love. He is divine energy. We are part of the trinity of **love, light, and energy.** Our energy is our spirit. The energy part never dies, (only changes form-physics law) because the spirit lives on. The spirit is the part of us that never dies. God is the light. And, we are starlight. We are part of that universal mind. The Christ consciousness.

God is love or the vibration of love in the form of compassionate thoughts or emotions. We express god when our thoughts are free of judgement and fear. And our behavior follows. Keeping our thought forms pure and free of judgement requires work though. I find myself asking the great spirit, or my higher self to help me adhere to these beliefs. It is not always easy in today's world. Prayer or meditation is important to help us keep our thought forms pure.

In other words, ask the great spirit god or your higher self to help you achieve this very important idea of purifying your thoughts. No matter how bad a situation may be, there is always something to be grateful for. That's where the focus must be. Meditation is the idea of going within to that point of consciousness where god individualizes in us.

A very wise man said that "If you change the way you think of something the thing you think of changes." If we don't like how things are, we have to change the way we think and feel about a situation and the situation will change.

I think that Jesus wanted to teach us to love and forgive. Somewhere along the line that information has been altered from its original message of love and forgiveness. The alteration of the original message has allowed and endorsed war and torture and man's inhumanity to man in the name of god for a long time.

I believe the secret societies are the powers that be, and I believe they are aliens or have alien blood or alien connections. And they have influenced religious doctrines. Some of these religious leaders have access to so much money they could alleviate the problems of the poor. And some of these religious leaders that build these mega churches should perhaps build places for the homeless to live instead. We are our brothers' keepers. It seems to me that the super-rich (top 1%) should embrace that concept, and then there would be no homeless and hungry. If they can throw millions in the toilet and never miss it, then perhaps it's up to those that can help without lowering their own level of comfort to do so. If they can design policies that pay for wars to continue, and spend billions on weapons, then they can take care of the people in need of the very basics. Unless it is in their best interest to withhold money, by designing laws and policies that ensure struggle and suffering. Simply because this negative energy feeds them.

I believe that the powers that be invented the idea of Capitalism. Capitalism provides the environment whereby greed can be expressed. We all fall victim to this piece of tender called money. Too many people struggle most of their lives to put a roof over their heads and feed their families. For so many people the chaos of everyday life is very stressful. And the stress is deadly. It kills lots of folks on a regular basis. High blood pressure is a big (silent) killer. No worries though because big pharma has a drug for you, they got the solution. They got your back, NOT. But be sure to read the warning!!! For example, the familiar quote I hear on television commercials pushing pharmaceuticals, "should you experience dizziness, loss of breath, etc... **Contact your physician**. And, you can be sure he has a drug for that problem.

I have truly come to believe that there is a diabolical plan by the powers that be. These individuals that run world politics, create wars etc.. and (promote New World Order) So, my thoughts are that these individuals that perpetuate the insane world that we are experiencing actually feed off of the energy created by the fearful thoughts taking place in so many folks' minds. I can't even imagine the fear that people who are experiencing war, as we speak, are going through.

Could there be certain beings that create chaos, because they feed off of the energy of (fear) that war, and the struggle to survive creates. It seems that whenever there is a peaceful leader who does not endorse war, they are either killed or silenced.

I recently was watching Ancient Aliens series on TV. The documentary was discussing the idea that human beings were perhaps genetically altered to be workers, to mine gold. Apparently, they (aliens) needed gold to keep their species alive. Or, could it be that they needed something for us to slave over (mining) just to create the energy that feeds them. I can't think of a worse job than that of going underground and being a minor.

Having said that, it reminds me of the Pink Floyd's song (Us and Them) the lyrics go like this, "**us us us and them them them, and after all we are just ordinary men.**" The video that is related to the song demonstrates in such a visual way how there are those that call the shots and there are those that follow along like good people. Or are we sheeple.

In the video it shows how we **Us Us Us** are marching off to war and, it shows men entering the darkness of the mines to work and toil as miners. But, by comparison the video shows **them them them** (politicians), enjoying golf and the finer things in life while the masses are toiling to feed their families, and hoping to get ahead. The words to that song are self-explanatory to me. There is us and there is them. My interpretation is that there are human beings (us) and the top 1% or 2 % (them). We are just ordinary men and they are not ordinary men perhaps they are not men at all perhaps they are aliens. That is my take anyway.

There are many ways that the powers that be distract us from the issues that plague us as a people of planet earth. If we are not the type of people that are likely to break the law by using street drugs, that's not a problem. There are numerous pharmaceuticals available that are legal but cause just as much chaos and pain as the street drugs. We have numerous prescription drugs available, that were introduced by the powers that be. Oh yes what-ever the issue, there is a drug to make you feel better for a minute. Big pharma has that one covered. Oh, but be careful because the powers that be have designed laws that will put you in jail if you fall into the trap of self- medicating, to ease the pain of our struggle to survive in a sick world. I read a joke where the doctor tells the patient take this prescription and don't worry if the drug doesn't address the issue because the side effects are far worse than the original issue, and you are sure to forget about the original issue.

There are so many ways we self-medicate in an effort to ease the struggle of surviving in a chaotic world. However, there is sure to be a law to get us in trouble if we do take advantage of the alcohol or illicit drugs that are available. How ironic that we can drive to a bar conveniently located throughout the city. But don't get caught leaving that bar with alcohol in your system. It's as if they set you up. It's also crazy that alcohol has been legal and it's a struggle to legalize weed, which is proven to be good medicine. I can see why the powers that be would not want us smoking the peace pipe loaded with pot. Smoke pot and the last thing you want to do is fight. It's hard for the powers that be to get their war on if people are smoking the peace pipe. We saw much opposition to war in the peace and love generation. I remember the Kent State University shooting. The National Guard were authorized to open fire on unarmed students protesting war. It's hard to believe that this happened. 3 unarmed students were killed in this protest.

If we are busy then we have no time to wonder why things are the way they are. We have been conditioned to be good people, we just go along like sheeple and question nothing. We are just happy to have a couple days every week, to be with family, to relax and recuperate from the hassles of the work week. That would include for many, the drive to and from work, (traffic). And the stress of making ends meet. People just want to relax on their days off and rest and have enough left over on their checks to do something enjoyable even if it's just to buy a six pack, or a little herb to help them relax and unwind. They are happy to have some rest till Monday comes along and start all over again. Sadly, there are many folks that never even get a day off, working two jobs does not allow it.

CHAPTER 34

NATIVES WERE TARGETED

I was watching my favorite news show. It is on a public television station (there are no commercials driving this news show). This broadcast has no ties or influence by corporations. They were covering the fact that the Native tribes from all over the country are uniting to keep the Dakota access pipeline from possibly contaminating the water. It seems to me things have come full circle. The Native Americans who were the keepers of the earth are once again facing the powers that be. I want to point out once again that the earth, the air, the water and the food has all been compromised for the love of money, the root of all evil.

The money lovers are more concerned with lining their pockets than ensuring that their children and grandchildren have clean water and food to consume. It's as if they have another place to go after they destroy this planet. Perhaps they do. The powers that be have no love or respect for this planet or the masses of people that inhabit the earth. Their behavior is inhumane. Maybe they are not human at all. Perhaps they are not from this planet at all.

The united states broke just about every treaty that was ever made with the native Americans, they then herded the natives to reservations, on to land that no one wanted. Now they want to build a pipeline which will help to further the destruction of our mother earth and her resources. It's time we all stand with the Native Americans on behalf of mother earth and her resources. Water is life. Without water there is not life. And it's time we demand that policy makers look more seriously at other ways of fueling this planet. Including and especially hemp and solar, and wind power.

While I am on the subject of water, I want to remind people of the fact that human beings are comprised of 80 to 90% water. Some say 75% water, in any case we are mostly made up of water. We should all participate in helping the Native Americans protect the water simply because water **is** life. And I have heard it said, that we should be careful what we say because our cells are listening. Now I understand why. If thoughts can affect water by turning it into different shapes, based on the type of thoughts, as I witnessed in the movie that explained quantum physics to me. The documentary I watched made a strong case for the idea that our thoughts and emotions create our reality. The demonstration showed how loving thoughts affect the shape of water droplets. Loving thoughts directed at the water droplets, by monks produced sacred geometric shapes. Conversely, the water droplets assumed very uneven unattractive shapes when focused on by haters. If our thoughts create our reality, and effect matter as demonstrated with the water droplets, then it's important for us to keep our thoughts pure and of a high vibration.

I believe that our aura is perhaps a reflection of the frequency at which we vibrate. And, since we are 80 to 90% water, just imagine how our thoughts and emotions and words affect us, since we are made up of mostly water. It's so important for us to keep our thought forms pure and positive. Our thoughts and emotions can affect our health. I believe that this is why it is said that our attitude effects our health. We should all have an attitude of gratitude. That's a good way to start the morning off. Thank the great spirit or god or the universe for this day. Count your blessings. It sets the mood for the day.

Native Americans knew that we are all one. And they plan their life around that idea. In other words. Knowing that we are all one with all that is, gave them a profound respect for nature and everything was sacred to them. As I said before many tribes did not even pick food from the vine without giving thanks and praise. As I pointed out they were intuitive about many things.

Native Americans were very intuitive about many things. One reason is because of their use of earth drugs to gain spiritual knowledge. For example, the use of **peyote** in a spiritual manner allowed the user to **see** energy under certain circumstances. And, it became apparent when one can see energy, that there is no place where you begin and I end. It's possible to see we are all connected. It's like we are all this soup of energy, and when one can see energy in this way, It was just obvious for natives to conclude that we are all one.

If one can see energy, then it becomes apparent that there is no place where I begin and you end. It's like we are all this soup of energy. it was just an obvious conclusion for natives to deduce that we are all one. And knowing that fact, they expanded on it by using collective thought and energy to bring about the reality that they wanted to occur. For example, Sundance brought sun, rain dance brought rain. So, my understanding would lead me to believe that if Native Americans brought rain or sun that in those cases, they certainly reached a **critical mass**.

The peace pipe was also part of the Native Americans spiritual rituals. And it did promote a more peaceful society. Natives never fought wars for some deep dark political objective. And since money had not been introduced to the American continent, there were no money lovers like the super-rich today. The root of all evil is the love of money. And I would have to conclude that capitalism, or any form of government based on money or capital will always lead to the money lovers expressing greed, and untimely separation.

Capitalism provides the atmosphere whereby greed can be expressed. It's no wonder that the powers that be with their diabolical plan would take away the peace pipe and make it unlawful to smoke weed. However, they had no problem introducing alcohol. And, we all know that natives (and others) can-not handle alcohol. The whites of their eyes turn yellow, and I have seen lots of people get crazy after drinking alcohol. They don't call it fire water for nothing. I have seen alcohol have a negative effect on many people from all walks of life, some get violent, especially, if they have anger issues. They don't call it spirits for nothing. Alcohol can bring in the bad spirits for sure.

The powers that be are so good at introducing destructive chemicals into our world. And, they are good at targeting the people who most threaten them. Natives American's entire existence involved their spiritual beliefs. Everything was sacred to them. As I pointed out before even picking fruit from the vine involved prayer. In order for the powers that be to ultimately be able to direct world politics in the direction that we find ourselves heading towards, they had to destroy Natives spirituality and force upon them religion. And now, it's commonly accepted that we are allowing our mother earth to be exploited. The number of trees needed to supply all the fast food products with paper goods to serve their products is astounding. And we continue to allow the rain forest to be cut down for these purposes, as well as other purposes. The Native Americans were the keepers of the earth and they had to be reduced to living on reservations. Their spiritual beliefs were taken from them. Their medicine bags were taken from the shaman which contained the herbs they used for healing and enlightenment. They then gave them alcohol. Part of the native spirituality embodied the idea of mother earth being sacred. Now, without the spiritual keepers of the earth, money takes precedence over mother earth. Now days people act as if money is sacred.

I read that one of the first religious priests to observe the Sioux tribe, said "these people live the bible and they have never even seen it." I am assuming he meant the good parts of the bible that promote love. The Sioux tribe referred to their journey through life as walking the red road. This meant that they thought highly of being good people and tried to live their lives as good human beings. I have attended modern day sun dance. The folks that attend for spiritual reasons often times fast. They do without food and often times water and dance in the sun. I believe in this way it is possible to connect with the sun in much the same way as I did while meditating on my picnic table when I experienced a million pin point light bulbs going off in my head. They become one with the sun or the light. And, many tribes believe god is the sun and call god the great spirit or Tonkashula.

I'm not religious I consider myself spiritual. I have been to hell, here on earth. Religious people are afraid of going to hell. Spiritual people have been there. I take issue with parts of various religious ideas that promote war and endorse doctrines that place women as second class. However, I do honor those parts of the bible that demonstrate great love. I have come to realize that God is pure energy, and light and love when expressed through us. I believe Jesus was sent here to demonstrate what great love can do. He taught of love and forgiveness. And I believe that Jesus vibrated on such a frequency that he could walk on water. I do pick and choose those parts of the bible that I think shed light and wisdom and allow me to understand the 11/11 phenomena. The reason I do pick and choose statements from the bible is because they resonate with me, and support the position I have assumed throughout this book. And since I have read several books that do not necessarily align themselves with conventional religious doctrines, I have become ever more discerning.

The best documentary I have ever watched is the one called 500 Nations. I learned that some tribes never had a word for war. **The Tieena,** were such people. On the other hand, there were native tribes that fought other tribes when food stores were low and, there were very clear reasons why the natives fought in battle, to preserve food stores for the tribe to survive the winter for example. They did not war for some deep dark political objective, that no one clearly understood. I was brought up to fear the Russians in the 1950's, yet I did not know one Russian to actually hate or fear.

I believe Native Americans understood quantum physics without naming it. Quantum physics makes a strong case for the idea that our thoughts create our reality. And I believe that our collective thoughts create our collective reality. They knew that if they needed sun for example, the whole village would collectively do sun dance by focusing their energy (thoughts) by praying for sun, they knew that they could in fact bring the sun out with this method. And they also knew that we are all connected in other words they knew we are all One. And they planned their life around that idea. In other words, knowing that we are all one gave them a profound respect for mother earth, nature, and everything on earth. They believed that everything has a life has a spirit has a name. They demonstrated this belief, in that everything was sacred to them. They referred to god as the great spirit. Many tribes did not even pick food from the vine without giving thanks and praise to the fruit tree that supplied them with nourishment.

CHAPTER 35

TRUE ALCHEMY

Going within as in meditation is one way of keeping us in touch with the light and love that dwell within. The temple of god is within. In this way the thoughts of love that produce kindness and compassion become automatic, when dealing with everyday life scenarios. It's hard often time to implement responses that reflect our beliefs. Our response, to the difficult scenarios that we find ourselves dealing with is very important. We are systematically bombarded by the powers that be with negative energy caused by fear, lack of resources, and various other stressors put upon us. In other words, meditation helps us respond to stress in a more positive way. It's not what happens to you it's how you deal with it that matters. Meditation helps us get in touch with the god within, within all of us. This connection helps to rid us of fear and helps us deal with life.

I like to quiet my mind in meditating rather than speaking, because there is nothing, I can tell god that he does not already know.

My spiritual teachers encourage the idea of meditation to combat negative thought, so I too, ask the great spirit to purify the thought forms that come into my head. I am a firm believer in meditation, because it drives home, many of the spiritual points that are so hard to live by in the world. We all know what's right. We all know we should not judge one another or be hateful or say mean things. We are bombarded with a world full of negative energy, so meditation is a means or tool to combat the negative. Meditation is a process where one goes within to that point in consciousness where God individualizes in all of us, because the temple of God does lie within all of us.

It is difficult to combat all the negative energy that takes place in our world today. We need spiritual food. It takes a conscientious effort to be in a place where our perceptions automatically begin coming from a place of love or non judgement. A place where love is the default mode, and our responses come from that mode. The shift in perception can take place when we ask for help from the great spirit or our higher selves or god or the universe or whoever you pray to. Ask and you shall receive. When the shift in perception occurs it actually makes you see things differently. When you come to a situation with purified thoughts, this is a manifestation of a shift in perception. The shift allows one to direct any scenario to a more positive direction. I have learned, that it is not what happens to you, but how you will react that matters. This is **true alchemy**. Turn our hearts from lead to gold. **This is where the magic is.**

If my thought forms are free of judgement, and are coming from love, then situations and issues progress on a more positive note, if we are confronted with a situation that might be perceived as a negative by one person may well perceived as an opportunity by another person when confronted with the same scenario. It depends on how we look at something. It depends on how we perceive the scenario. Our perception will determine how we react. It's not what happens to you, it's how you react, that determines how the scenario will unfold.

At one time I found myself living with my sibling. He has since passed away. He had been a drug addict most of his life. He had caused so much heartache and pain to our family, that I resented him. He had become disabled and dependent on me for assistance in many ways. He had transgender issues which I am sure contributed to his drug abuse. It was the fact that he was so needy, together with the resentments I had regarding him, that did not allow me to give him the care he needed without being resentful. My intentions were not coming from love. By now my brother had become my sister. That did not bother me. In fact, his size and looks did not make his attempts to be feminine very believable. I always felt sorry for him regarding his appearance as a female. He was a very handsome male, as a female not so much. I knew that I had to get rid of my resentments. All my life I had watched my mom and dad enable him to do drugs. They were constantly throwing him money, hoping it would end the insanity of his drug abuse. They were always so angry and resentful that they just fed the problem. I am sure he only felt their anger even as he readily took the money, they threw at him and the problem.

I knew that I could not live with him (her) without getting rid of the resentments. I had a real hard time dealing with needs without showing resentment which I know she often felt. One particular morning, I was doing my meditation, and I heard her making her way to the restroom. I got a sense of dread at the prospect of dealing with her this day. I knew I needed help implementing love while caring for her needs. I knew I needed help giving her love while tending to her needs. I knew I needed help to get rid of the resentments. I wanted to give her care with love. I asked god, the universe, my higher power to take away the resentment so that I could tend to her needs with love. Unlike my parents who were always so angry. They tended to her but not with love.

As I was meditating and asking for help, I was asking god please help me tend to my sister in a loving manner. It was instantaneous, I was instantly relieved of the resentments that I was burdened with for so many years. It was a shift that took place instantaneously. Ask and ye shall receive. It was magic. True alchemy.

CHAPTER 36

PARANORMAL OCCURRENCES

I'd like to say that I think certain events in my life brought me to the point where I was open to paranormal phenomena. And, I actually think that meditation makes you more vulnerable to that type of vibration being able to cross over into your particular vibrational-frequency or a frequency that resonates with you would be a better description.

Prior to my son's death, several events occurred that led me to have a strong belief that there is a spirit world and they do communicate. My first experience was a dream from the spirit-world. My friend and neighbor died suddenly, and shortly after her death I had this dream about her. In my dream, I was observing her funeral and as they were carrying her casket down this deep stairway, they dropped her and she fell out the casket, but this whole scenario was under the umbrella of humor because when they dropped her she sat up and in the most harsh like voice, which was so easily to identify as hers, she said what the hell are you guys doing, it was so funny. I remember waking up at that point and I was laughing out loud because it was just like her to give me a funny dream to let me know that there is a spirit world and they can communicate, and it wasn't scary.

My son and I encountered an unusual occurrence together. When he was small, we lived way out in the country. We were on our way home the little store a few miles from our house. The road was very dark and secluded, and there were no street lights. I was driving on the road headed towards home with my son. Suddenly, what appeared to be a very Casper like figure came down from above us and floated in front of the windshield. I had slowed way down, to observe this unusual apparition, and this little white transparent ghost like figure floated in front of our windshield just as slow as you please, and as it passed by my side of the windshield, it looked directly at me with black eyes, and floated back up into the trees and disappeared. The only thing I can say about this occurrence, and what effect it may have had on my future was to impress upon me and my son, the idea that there is a spirit world and my son, and I now knew it. And it wasn't necessarily something to be feared, but it did exist.

I want to share this incident. My youngest grandson and I were driving along the road, my grandson's phone made a noise that prompted him to look at his cell phone. The time was on his cell was 4:11, my son's birthday. We were surprised when we looked up and noticed the truck ahead of us was a truck that had my son's name across the top (Seth). Wow what a co-incidence or rather synchronicity. I believe that my son wanted us to know that he was with us that day.

Another synchronicity I experienced with (my youngest grandson) occurred while walking my youngest grandson to the bus stop. This particular event happened not long after my mother had passed away, as grandson and I were on our merry way to the bus stop, we noticed a leaf doing odd things as we walked passed a tree in our path. So odd in fact that we stopped and turned around and began to observe the leaf as it seemed to be performing for us. It began to go up and down and side to side and it was so unbelievable that I kept looking for a string. This went on for a couple of minutes, it was amazing to see a leaf doing the things it was doing. I feel as though this was my mom's spirit letting us know, that her spirit is with us, and it was magical.

I had another incident occur when I was taking my usual walk around the complex where I worked. Something caught my attention and I looked up. There was a leaf in the tree above. The leaf had a piece of cotton or something on it but it was fluttering like a boxer's punching bag, and, there was no other leaf moving. But this time I was able to catch part of it on my cell phone camera.

Another incident I remember well, occurred on my first day of massage therapy class. I had found my seat and I was looking around my new classroom. I looked up to see a young man with my son's name on his ball shirt and when he turned around, I saw he had an 11 on his shirt it was his athletic number in big letters. Wow, what a co-incidence, or synchronicity. He had the same name as my son, and his ball shirt had number 11 on it.

After my mother died, I began to go to school for massage therapy. Going to school limited my income because I could only work part time. I remember telling my mom before she passed on, I said " Mom, when you cross over will you give me a sign, so I know you're in heaven." She said without hesitation, in the most nonchalant manner, "I suppose so if I can." And she did.

It happened in this way, shortly after mom's death. I lived next door to mom and dad prior to mom's death, and after I remained living next door to daddy. I remember I was sweeping between the house trailers, and dad came down the steps of his trailer house and said I had a visit from your mom last night, in a dream. He said your mom told me, "Help your daughter" He said "I know your sister, doesn't need help so I know she meant you." And, he was right. I had burned myself out at all the corporations, because I had tried to start a union at one of the corporations where I worked, and word got around. And, I was black balled. And that is when I decided to go back to school for massage. And my dad said he would help me financially. What a blessing my mom and dad were.

My mom died at home and she let us know that her spirit was still around. It happened in this way. Mom had a particular perfume that she loved. After she passed, the scent of her perfume lingered on her pillow for at least a month after she crossed over. Her scent also lingered in the air around the house that she died in, we could smell her scent as we drove up to the house, she let us know that her spirit was with us.

At the time all this took place I was doing some automatic writing in the form of poetry and I was super involved in bringing awareness of the impending plan to bomb Iraq. I simply couldn't imagine adding more negative energy by way of fear, to our shared world. Especially because my belief in the concept regarding fear and love. I think that automatic writing is a demonstration of a paranormal occurrence. This poem came to me while my spirit was so immersed in the idea of the possibility of more war and more bombs and killing etc... I wrote the poem that I named " Weapons of Mass Construction."

CHAPTER 37

DENVER INTERNATIONAL AIRPORT

I think that there is hidden meaning in much of the art work at the DIA, that I must introduce, because it is so relevant to our current experience. There is a lot of mystery surrounding the Denver International airport, and its artwork. And there are some interesting mural paintings on some of the walls within the airport. The airport was built on a Native American spiritual burial ground. It is said that there are deep underground tunnels that run under the airport and all the way to NORAD and perhaps throughout the U.S. It is also interesting to note that there is mysterious, if not sinister, artwork there. The murals and a statue that are quite interesting and perhaps even revealing to the discerning eye.

From Ariel photography, it is interesting to note that the runways at Denver international airport, are designed to form a swastika. Upon approaching the airport by car, one will see the infamous, anatomically correct huge statue of a blue bronco with red eyes that light up. It's standing erect in a challenging position, exposing male genitalia. This statue is often referred to as Lucifer, or (Blucifer.) because of its sinister look as well as the fact that the man who was contracted to construct the huge statue was killed when the statue fell on him.. His son had to finish the project. I think they, (them them them - powers that be) are trying to connect the bronco with the football team by the same name, to throw a person off with regard to the sinister implications of the statue. Most people are aware of the Denver Co. football team.

I think it's wonderful and amazing that people can be brought together with one idea in mind. That is to say many people look forward to football season because it's fun to watch the game with your family and friends. It's a great way of passing the time and rooting for your favorite team. It's a demonstration of how people love to gather for fun and common goals. I bet we could change the course of the world if we gathered with that much enthusiasm towards world peace. I think it totally made a difference during the Viet Nam war. I think all the energy directed towards opposition to war, by so many people during that war, was instrumental in putting an end to it. Opposition came in various forms. So many of the songs were focused on the idea of peace, love and social justice. I don't think anything touches the heart and soul of people like music. The vibration of heart felt songs that came from people of that era, was instrumental in driving the opposition.

I do want to remind people that football is another way of distracting the masses, the Romans used the same method of distraction with the gladiator games. Keep them entertained, distracted. The use of the games by the powers that be is in a sense sinister just as Lucifer the statue implies, with its red eyes that are always lit up. The man who was contracted to make the statue was crushed by the statue while working on it. Apparently his son had to finish it. I choose to see the positive aspects of the game though. There is good and bad in everything. I see how much fun people have when they gather to root for their favorite team and become one for a common goal.

It's not that its bad to watch football, play video games, television etc... but my thoughts are there should be a balance of energies with regard to pastimes. In other words, sometime should be spent on a collective level with focus on world peace. I wish there was a world leader who could unite all the people the way Ghandi did for the common goal of achieving justice and equality for all. He did so and demanded that it be done peacefully.

CHAPTER 38

THE ODD ARCHITECTURAL DESIGN

The airport has an odd architectural design. There are odd shaped canopies for lack of a better word. These canopy type structures actually look like crooked tipis from a distance. And there is a dark band around the top of some of the tipi looking structures. At first glance it reminds me of the head gear worn by some Arabs. Some people think it resembles the Kul Klux Klan's hoods. And the fact that the tipi looking structures are crooked, is symbolic (to the awaken mind) of disrespect, towards Native Americans. As I stated before Natives were targeted. Mostly because of their spiritual beliefs. We can't have people whose spiritual beliefs embody the idea of mother earth being sacred and the water as well. In fact, the choice to build the airport on Native American spiritual burial grounds is truly symbolic of disrespect towards the native peoples.

What do you make of it?

The fact that the decision has been made to go ahead with the Dakota access pipeline is an indication of disrespect for the land and the water and the keepers of these things, (Native Americans). And I believe the artwork and the designers of the airport artwork are alluding to the fact that natives and Arabs, as being the unfortunate pawns in the diabolical scheme that the aliens or powers that be have planned out.

It is a cruel and unusual way of making fun of our inability to see through the game that they have unleashed upon humanity. The continued war with the Arab world by interfering in the Middle East with our support of Israel. This idea endorsed in the Bible. And the continued disrespect of the Native Americans. The result is that the earth, the air, the water and the food have all been compromised for the root of all evil. Natural healing is discouraged in favor of Big Pharma. They always have their war on somewhere. The war game that gambles with our children lives in a game that has no rules. That line from another song from the stream of consciousness that came from Laurel Canyon. John Phillips wrote the words and Scott Mackenzie sang it. Magic took place at Laurel Canyon. I have heard of the invasion of the new world (Americas) referred to as manifest destiny. The dark plan to unleash money, religion and technology on America (the New World). The Native Americans did not have money. The powers that be knew that all three would cause chaos. There is no balance when we no longer have respect for mother earth. Native spirituality had to be destroyed by destroying the native people. The keepers of the earth had to be silenced, with war and genocide. And the destiny that has come to fruition is what we are experiencing.

Within the airport is at least one placard that states **New World airport commission.** There are also statues of gargoyles at the airport. I want to mention that on the 100th year anniversary of Geronimo's death, his heirs sued the secret societies charging that some of its members robbed

Geronimo's grave in 1918 and took possession of his skull and have kept it in a glass case ever since. How weird is that? I have heard it said that the powers that be, (secret societies) are known to groom 15 Yale students a year for politics. And it is said that they have ceremonies in the building referred to as the tomb at Yale.

Possessing Geronimo's skull is perhaps a trophy and symbolic of the idea that the invaders of this continent were successful in taking away native spiritual beliefs and the idea that everything was sacred. Geronimo fought white settlers and the Mexican army and United States army for 3 decades, before surrendering. He was the last of the great warriors. Perhaps his skull is a symbol of accomplishment, and the idea that the powers that be finally succeeded in subduing Native American spiritual beliefs. And, replacing the native spiritual belief that mother earth was sacred, with the idea that money is sacred instead. It's in your wallet, it's on our money, in God we trust.

The powers that be also used alcohol to further destroy the natives. At one time there were 500 tribes. War, disease and genocide has succeeded in reducing the numbers considerably. I admire the offspring of the natives who fought for this land. They are still protesting the Dakota pipeline, along with vets and other concerned citizens of planet earth. And, of course money did not exist on this continent before the invasion. These diabolical beings knew that capitalism provides the environment whereby greed can be expressed, and the money lovers (them) have no problem expressing their greed, and cruelty towards humans leaving me to once again question if they are full blooded humans. And, withholding money and promoting war and poverty are just some of the ways that they create the energy of fear needed to feed these beings.

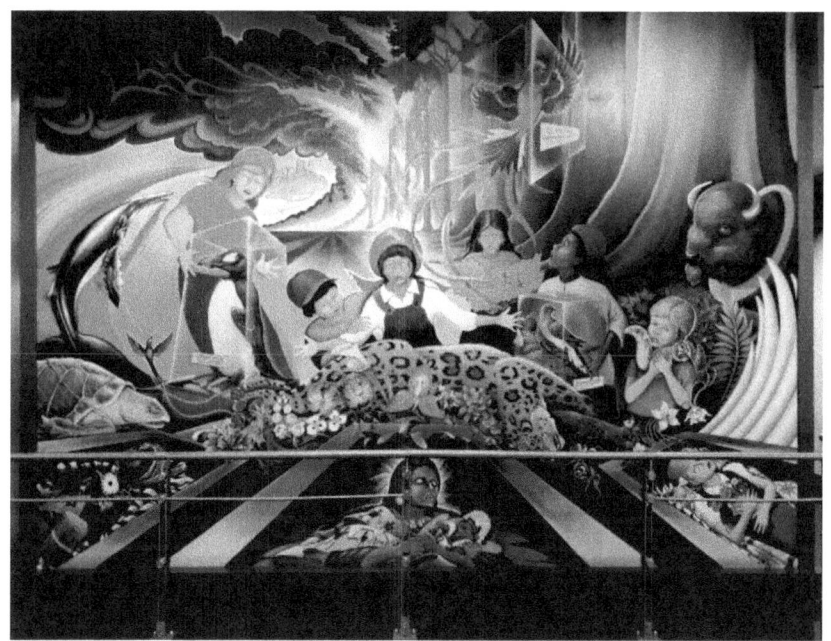

The huge mural picture that first caught my eye was the one where 3 females are in coffins. A black woman, a native American woman, and a white girl. All in coffins. In the background is what appears to be chaos, fire and destruction. Much like the chaos of the photo depicts extinction of birds. This particular picture is, in my mind a symbol of feminine energy being kept down. This imbalance of energy sets the stage for war to be perpetuated.

Another mural is of a figure resembling an alien or perhaps a (Nazi) with a huge sword striking down the bird of peace. In the background is a dim partial rainbow. And it appears to be brown women weeping in the mural, while the buildings in the background are war torn and blown in half. This mural reminds me of the idea that aliens are opposed to peace, or rather in my mind the energy that would exist in a peaceful world. And people of color are particularly affected by the chaotic aftermath depicted in the picture. As in the case of the Native American. For they were keepers of the earth. And since the European invasion, the earth, the air, the water, and the food has all been compromised for the root of all evil. I find it odd that the runway at DIA is in a swastika. The U.S. government brought German scientists here after WWII. This was called Operation Paperclip. These two facts together with the photo makes the awakened mind question the motives of those who would do these things.

Another mural depicts a type of flower in the center of the mural, and there is illumination around the flower. The people around it appear to be flocking towards the center where the illuminated flower is. This picture reminds me that the natives gained enlightenment through their use of peyote and other plants that are known to be instrumental for enlightenment, when used in a spiritual manner, particularly in the Native American world, at least on our continent. As I stated before I believe that natives acquired respect for mother earth, and the knowledge that we are all one, through the ingestion of various spiritual earth drugs. Or, another interpretation that's looks plausible with regard to this particular mural, is that the illumination is coming from a lotus flower. It seems plausible because a lotus is symbolic of coming out of darkness into the light. A lotus grows out of the darkness of muddy waters to become the beautiful lotus flower. Or the various colors in the center of the illumination could be symbolic of chakras being awakened. In any case all of the interpretations seem to have one thing in common and that is illumination or enlightenment.

My favorite mural is one where people from all over the world are together with a full-on rainbow above all of them. And they are all holding signs of peace in various languages. And, in the middle of all the people is a person holding a **guitar**. Perhaps this is symbolic of the idea that the vibration of **music** and the collective gathering of like-minded people, can create this scenario of peace depicted in this picture. And most interestingly at the bottom of the picture is the alien (Nazi) type figure that was pictured in the other mural striking the dove of peace. In this particular picture the bird is on top of the alien who is laying on the ground. Could this picture be an indication that we can achieve peace if we are all one with the **intention** of bringing about peace. I think it is.

Could it be that the powers that be actually put the truth for us to see in a puzzle, encrypted in a way that can only be deciphered by those who have their third eye open. Or those who vibrate at a frequency that allow for them to decipher certain encryptions and codes or those who are open to alternative ideas, and question the status quo. It seems there are so many clues to the puzzle given by both sides of the fear versus love equation. I certainly received my awakening code. But it would seem only fair that those who have been manipulated by the powers that be (as we all have been) would be given the choice of free will. Perhaps the mathematical formula that I explained earlier in the book (regarding people's birthdates) is an indication of free will. As I explained everyone ends up with 111, after doing the little mathematical formula, relating to their birthdates. The 1 that is missing, would be determined by our choices and the choice would complete the gate, or pathway that is created by the completion or the 11 by adding the missing 1. The choice of living out of fear or love. But there are none so blind as those that see and will not. Wake up sheeple the hawks are ever present.

If one studies the murals as I have, it's possible to see a story emerging from all the murals. It would appear to me that if we are all together as one, and our intention is that of peace, like the mural with the full rainbow, that we can change our current reality, into a peaceful one. I have been reminded by so many people that there will always be wars. Perhaps that is true on this particular realm of existence. By that I mean if that is how they think, then that is the reality they will create, along with others that think that way. Perhaps the yin yang theory of good and bad, black and white, war and peace, often referred to as duality, will always exist on this dimension, or this realm of existence. As I stated before, we as humans are the ground for the two energies of positive and negative. It is up to each and every one of us to rid ourselves of ego, and have the dark night of the soul and work on purifying our thoughts individually, since our thoughts create our reality. Our thoughts have been shaped or conditioned by the information that we have been force fed by the school system and religion and the media. When they own the information they can bend it all they want. Our reality has been shaped by our perceptions which have been hijacked by a sinister group of elite beings. Perhaps if enough of us choose to have their thought forms come from love instead of fear which is the current default mode of the masses, we could change our reality. We have been conditioned to react out of fear not love. It's time for those of us that are concerned about the world today should take an active part in changing the collective reality we share.

Perhaps it is possible to change our reality collectively by reaching a critical mass of people choosing to love over fear. Maybe we could vibrate to a higher dimension on a collective level once critical mass is reached. After having said that I am reminded of the disappearance of the Mayan Indians. I have often thought that perhaps they were questioning the idea of sacrificing for the gods. I believe that what they believed to be the gods descending from the sky was in fact an alien ship. Perhaps they were questioning the idea of sacrifice. Perhaps that is how they disappeared. Maybe they reached a critical mass of people that were focusing on another reality such as a reality where they did not have to sacrifice for the sake of the gods, who demanded sacrifice. A reality without the fear of possibly being a victim of such a barbaric act as sacrifice.

I have for a long time thought it would have to be the women who would bring about a big change. I believe that because it's the women who for centuries have been silenced by the powers that be. The concept of the sacred feminine was that there was a matriarchal culture in early religions, and supposedly the church under Constantine attempted to crush it. As we look back on history it seems to be repeating itself. I believe we have arrived at a place where the violence and disharmony within the collective of mankind and the destruction against Gaia Sophia (one of the spirit names for our mother earth) poses a serious threat to our lives on this planet.

I want to tell you that there are those of us who see the value of not being under the influence of money and religion or technology. There are those of us who have come to the point in life to where we don't need a lot to be happy. I have come to believe the more you own **the more it owns you**. I have no problem with those who desire more. If that is what they desire and have worked hard for all their lives to achieve, then they deserve to have those things. I respect someone who goes to school and works hard in an effort to bring about their desires. Or those who have worked hard and learned skills without the benefit of school. They deserve to have their desires come to fruition. For those folks I believe capitalism would work fine, but the money lovers the top one percent are the ones who ruin the idea of capitalism. They ruin it for those folks who would otherwise make capitalism work.

I want to point out that the **guitar** in the middle of the picture that depicts peace is symbolic of vibrations of sound as in the vibration of music. Symbolic of the importance of sound vibrations and the importance of making use of the universal language of music. I am reminded that the use of mantras like Ommm, are commonly used by meditators. Ommm means I am that I am that I am part of all that is. We are all part of the whole. "We are to the universe, as a wave is to the ocean." We are one and part of all there is.

I am reminded that, In the beginning was the Word, a vibration, the spoken Word, is a vibration. I defiantly think that music has a place in bringing us all together with loving vibrations of the frequency referred to as the god frequency. Or at least the emotions that the words bring out in us. I say this because so many of the songs of the 60's and 70's touched our hearts in a special way that only music can do. I think we need to be together. All as **one** with **the intentions** of bringing about a peaceful world with our collective vibrations. Keep in mind that Tesla said the secrets to the universe is energy, frequency and vibration. I'm reminded of another song that came after the 60's and 70's. It was intended to bring everyone together. The song "We are the world. We are the children." Random words such as "there's a choice were making were saving our own lives." These words seem to demonstrate the idea that the authors believed we are all one. The video of the song was very moving. The song pulls on the heart strings. Perhaps we need a resurgence of many of these special songs whose vibrations touch the heart in a special way.

In the mural with the guitar, I see a picture of many people from all over the world, with a full-on rainbow over them. They have achieved peace on a collective level. I see a picture of all god's children coming together as one. I see a guitar in the very center making it and its vibration, essential to the story. I am remembering all the while that there is a god vibration. and it's based on mathematical scales. I see at the bottom of the page the alien lying under the dove of peace.

So it would appear that if we are all in the zone (the vibrational frequency brought about by loving thoughts and musical sounds associated with the god vibrations, as well as songs with words that resonate with us and stir our emotions), that we can actually change our reality on a collective level. Since we are to the universe as a wave is to the ocean, a part of the whole, then it's possible to be an active and conscious part of what the universe is doing to promote peace across the globe. We could be the wave of change. Our current reality is a reflection of our collective thoughts born of fear. Love is what we are born with, fear is what we are taught.

The universe is speaking to us by way of synchronicities. Are you listening? The two gates symbolized by the 11 11 phenomena, are the two possible realities that could unfold when we are gripped by either thoughts of fear or loving thoughts. I also think that the idea of ones (1s) is symbolic of the importance of us being one at the same time, in an effort to change our current reality. In other words I think that it is essential that we all gather at least in our hearts and in our minds, our thoughts and pray collectively at synchronized times. Perhaps it might be even more effective to use the time, 11 11, so that we may all be on the same page at the same time using the mathematical symbols that the universe is giving those of us who are experiencing the 11 11 phenomena. And as I indicated earlier, the universe is addressing all of us by way of the mathematical formula that ends up 111 for everyone on the planet. I believe the universe is addressing all of us by way of the mathematical formula I laid out earlier. I believe that critical mass is relevant here. That is to say that if we have enough folks participating at the same time, we will reach a critical mass and that is the number needed to change our reality. Perhaps it's the 144,000 that is referred to in Revelations.

I am reminded of a more recent song by John Mayer. He does a great job in this song called **"Waiting for the World to Change"**. I picked random lines from the song that express many people's feelings.

> Now we see everything that's going wrong
> with the world and those who lead it
> now if we had the power
> to bring our neighbors home from war
> they would have never missed a Christmas
> no more ribbons on the door

I love the song, but I don't think we can wait for the world to change, we must be the change we wish to see. I believe it is time to **change** the world. It's time to be the change we wish to see. It is time to change the world we live in with our collective effort. It is time to face the dark night of the soul, forgive ourselves for our sins, knowing that we are both good and bad because that is how we manifest on this dimension. Therefore we must forgive all those that trespass against us, knowing that they manifest under the same conditions.

It appears to me that we have to set a time and date for all of us observers and anyone else who believes and wants to participate in our collective effort to gather at least in our hearts and minds at the **same time**. And it would be wonderful to gather together those that are able (much like the rainbow gathering, or Woodstock) with the vibrations of music, and our stirred emotions of love for each other and the planet, in an effort to bring about the paradise depicted in the Mayan temple of the descending gods. A reality based on collective thoughts of love. A reality brought about by naming our current collective experience as illusion, brought about by incorrect thoughts of fear. For all that truly exists is love.

The temple of god is within all of us. Namaste.

(WEAPONS OF MASS CONSTRUCTION, FREE, AND TALK TO ME HIPPIES)

Weapons of Mass Construction

Our weapon of choice must be

our collective spirituality

their weapon of choice

with all of their voice

was that of money, religion,

and technology

they came across the sea

to manifest destiny

to use religion to keep

down feminine energy

to create an imbalance

it's easy to see

and get rid of native spirituality

where everything was sacred indeed

take away the peace pipe

get rid of hopes of peace with one swipe

the top one percent use

cash as a tool

they express greed by withholding money

its evil and cruel

yes, money the love of which is

the root of all evil you see

they don't want anyone to be free

the love of money is the root of all evil

it's said, they want to keep all of their bread

when natives picked fruit from the vine

they gave thanks and praise every time

they knew how to use energy

their collective thoughts could bring rain

or sun can't you see

the rain dance was a sight to behold

it was way better than any gold

the diabolical ones indeed

spreading their European seed

they failed to see the flowers and

trees as important spiritual beings

just like you and me

they thought they owned what ever

land they landed on

the earth was just a dead thing

they could claim, but we know

every rock and tree and creature

has a life has a spirit has a name
it's called energy, constant rapid
random motion even if you can't see
the atoms that make up you and me
the only thing that can set us free
is the connection to god cant you see
the temple of god is within so I must
connect with that part of me
we have all been one from the beginning
one spirit with mother and each other
by now our bloods have been mixed
combined over a period of time
we must learn to forgive even them
for its time for the new age to begin
it's all down to you and me
brothers and sisters don't you see
we must bring our hearts and minds together
at the same time no matter the weather
we can make the world much better
we can do this at 11:11,
the sign is straight from heaven
I believe there are alien beings
I have been studying all of these things
they are running the world I am sure
they want to keep everyone poor
they want to keep everyone dumb
so, we can be under their thumb

they don't give a damn about the earth

to them our mother has no worth

there must be Martians indeed

they don't care and their tool is greed

the root of all evil indeed

their plan is really quite clear

to create chaos and fear

make sure we have plenty of beer

then we are easy to steer

if they can get us to stay mad

it really makes them feel glad

it opens the door for the bad

the fear they create

makes them feel great

it sure puts a lot on their plate

negative energy so strong

they can feast on it all year long

yes keep us living in fear

the opposite of love I hear

if their tool is greed and fear

then our path is really quite clear

we must beat them at their own game

show them we are one in the same

we are starlight not meant

to fuss and fight

together we can make it all right

we can create a new garden

I don't think it will be a problem
to end all the pollution
and defiantly stop all the shooting
a thousand years ago the Mayans predicted
every solstice, equinox, and moon eclipses
the bad aliens came from the sky
the Mayans thought they knew why
aliens demanded sacrifice from them
that's when the evil began
take them to the top of the pyramid shaped rock
scary alien faces carved in so many places
the pyramid is the symbol of the elite
it's something we can defeat
it's on our dollar as well
as far as I can tell we must reach a
critical mass so our collective spiritual
energy forces the evil to pass
when the Mayan Calendar ends
that's when the new age begins
the age of Aquarius its really up to us
when all the planets align
we will begin raising mass consciousness
at that time

FREE

All I want is to be free
to live off the land

can't you see
to not punch a clock
and in one week
get punked
by corporate evil and greed
man sows the devil's seed
and one of them is greed
imagine if we all just knew we were one
life would be so much fun
the lust for money isn't it funny
produces all the pain we see
if we could go back in time
in our hearts and in our minds
we could listen to reason
and rhyme
think of all the love
we could find
a time before money
the earth and her honey
was sacred to those that knew

TALK TO ME HIPPYS

talk to me hippys
the young and the old
all conscious people
who don't worship gold
talk to me hippy's

are your minds engaged

we still hate wars

and know they are staged

the new age revival

its for our survival

in the 60's we gathered

at Yasgur's farm

remember we

half a million strong

we proved at Woodstock

that we were all one

they said it was a fad

and it would soon be gone

the youth of today

you must carry it on

gathering together

under the sun

singing songs of peace

and beating that drum

the vibrations of love

that come from within

we must meditate

to keep us from sin

pray in our own way

every single day

we must open the gate

which will determine our fate

our future is dying

right before our faces

the god within will put us in our places

the things we are teaching

do not think we are preaching

we will see the faces

of those we are reaching

ABOUT THE AUTHOR

Christine is a licensed massage therapist, and energy worker and uses reiki and reflexology to help with the healing process. She incorporates crystals in her treatments. She also makes use of the pendulum. She explains how the pendulum is based on the same principal as divining rods. They are both tools. Those that use divining rods are referred to as water witches or diviners. They are good at finding where water exists underground by using divining rods. She uses the pendulum in a similar fashion to find issues in the body and treat them with energy work. The author has a background in the medical field and an associate of applied science degree. She has meditated for several years and believes that meditation has enhanced her healing abilities. She also believes that meditation has been instrumental in helping her to unravel the awakening code.

www.ingramcontent.com/pod-product-compliance
Lightning Source LLC
Chambersburg PA
CBHW071733120626
46550CB00002B/501